Boeing 757
Timelines

Nigel Richardson

First Edition 2024

ISBN 978 1 7398194 9 1

The information in this book is true and complete to the best of our knowledge. All recommendations are made without any guarantee on the part of the Publisher, who also disclaims any liability incurred in connection with the use of specific details or content within this book.

All rights reserved. No part of this book may be reproduced or transmitted in any form or by any means, electronic or mechanical, including photo-copying, scanning, recording or by any information storage and retrieval system, without permission from the Publisher in writing.

© 2024 Nigel Richardson

British Library Cataloguing-in-Publication Data
A catalogue record for this book is available from the British Library.

Published by Destinworld Publishing Ltd.
www.destinworld.com

Printed in India

Contents

Introduction		4
Chapter 1:	Origin, Design and Development of the 757	5
Chapter 2:	The 757 Described	16
Chapter 3:	Commercial Passenger Service	31
Chapter 4:	British Airways and the Boeing 757	47
Chapter 5:	Britain's last operator of passenger 757s: Jet2.com and the Boeing 757	56
Chapter 6:	The Flexible Freighter	63
Chapter 7:	The 757 as an Experimental Test Bed	73
Chapter 8:	Military and Government 757s	80
Chapter 9:	What next for the 757?	87
Appendix 1:	Boeing 757 Technical Specifications	92
Appendix 2:	Boeing 757 Orders and Deliveries	93
Appendix 3:	Boeing 757 Timeline	94
Bibliography		96

Acknowledgements

I would like to thank the following photographers and organisations for kindly allowing the use of their images in the book either directly or through Creative Commons: Bill Abbott, aceebee, Heather Anderson/Boeing, Roland Balik, Aero Icarus, aeroprints.com, Gabriel Mora Aldama, Pedro Aragão, Gerry Barron, Bidgee, BriYYZ, byeangel, Condor, contri, Colin Cooke, Tomás Del Coro, Curimedia, 2Excel, Matt Falcus, Ken Fielding, flybyeigenheer, Don Gilham, Felix Goetting, Kjell Oskar Granlund, Danny Grew, Sunil Gupta, Gerard Helmer, Gavin Hughes, Icelandair, Jet2.com, Kambui, Mike Kell, Adam Kress/Honeywell Aerospace, Sergey Kustov, Toby Lam, Sam Lockett, LRS747, Eddie Maloney, Pieter van Marion, Mike1979 Russia, Paul Miot-Paschke/Condor, N509FZ, NASA, New Zealand Defence Force, Martin Oertle, John Olafson, Michael Oldfield, Ahmed Orgunwall/Airlinercafe.com, Ewan Partridge, Pemco World Air Services, Adrian Pingstone, Pratt & Whitney, Shaun Psaila, Pseudopanax, Niclas Rebbelmund, Rockwell Collins, Javier Rodriguez, Rolls-Royce, Eric Salard, Julien.scavini, Juke Schweizer, Pertti Sipilä, SR-Planespotter, ST Engineering, Dan Stijovich, Jeroen Stroes Aviation Photography, Agil Suwandi, John Taggart, Clemens Vasters, John Visanich, Rolf Wallner, Cory W. Watts, wiltshirespotter, Mark Winterbourne, Zach Young/Precision Aircraft Solutions, Anna Zvereva. I would like to thank my wife, Gill, for carefully proof-reading each chapter of the book. Finally, my thanks to Matt Falcus and Destinworld Publishing.

Introduction

Once the Boeing 747 was introduced into service in 1970, Boeing began to consider further developments to its narrow-body aircraft, in particular looking to replace the Boeing 727-200. After a lengthy period of design studies which initially involved stretched derivatives of the Boeing 727, an all-new airliner finally emerged - the Boeing 757. At the same time, Boeing was developing a new wide-body aircraft - the Boeing 767. The aircraft manufacturer made the decision to develop these two very different airliners, aimed at contrasting markets, in tandem, treating them almost as a single programme. Hence, the 757 and 767 went on to share similar aerodynamic, structural and system features together with identical flight decks.

The Boeing 757 is a product of continuous design concepts and refinements (over a third of the final aircraft is the result of computer-aided design) and technological development. It is a significantly different design and product from previous Boeing jet airliners. The 757 has a distinctive blunter, rounded nose as opposed to the sharply pointed, snake-like nose section of the Boeing 707, 727 and 737. A new advanced technology wing design allowed for a reduction in the wing sweep to twenty-five degrees compared with the sharply swept wings of its predecessors. Construction of the aircraft includes a large amount of advanced composites and other lightweight materials which, when combined with the new, second-generation high by-pass turbofan engines, results in significant fuel savings and costs, thereby satisfying its customer's requirements. An advanced digital flight deck with cathode-ray tube colour displays and computerised systems replaced the more conventional electromechanical instruments in cockpits at the time.

Although the 757 wasn't one of the biggest selling airliners (only 1,049 aircraft had been built for customers when Boeing ended production in October 2004), it has proved popular with both passengers and flight crews. It has been particularly well suited to the less popular but viable transatlantic routes, usually to smaller, secondary airports. In the United States the 757 quickly became popular with passengers on transcontinental routes while in Europe it has transported many holidaymakers to Mediterranean destinations, contributing positively to their holiday memories. For flight crews, the 757's dependability, exceptional performance and handling characteristics have made it easy to operate, especially out of small airports. It also has an exemplary safety record.

The 757 still operates passenger services today, over four decades since it made its maiden flight, and its popularity as a cargo aircraft continues to grow. Aside from its commercial activities, the 757 also has military and VIP transport roles and, as a flying test bed, plays an important part in the development and testing of new aircraft systems and technologies.

The following chapters tell the story of the Boeing 757 from its evolution, design and development up to its entry into commercial passenger service. They describe the 757's career as a freighter and flying test bed as well as its operations for both government agencies and the military. The final chapter considers what the future may hold for this popular aircraft.

Chapter 1:

Origin, Design and Development of the 757

In the early 1970s Boeing established the New Aircraft Programme with the objective of designing some 'new generation' airliners to meet the needs of potential future market requirements. The new airliners would eventually replace or complement its current 707, 727, 737 and 747 aircraft. The 7X7 project, which evolved first, began as a short-haul aircraft development but the focus was shifted more towards fuel efficiency, longer range and greater passenger capacity following some airline feedback. The 7X7 project became a wide-body development proposed to fit between the 707 and 747, and went on to become the Boeing 767. Nevertheless, Boeing also decided to develop a single-aisle, narrow-body aircraft in parallel with the 7X7 and, in order to avoid the extortionate development costs of another entirely new airliner, Boeing explored the potential of a derivative of one of its existing aircraft, a stretched version of the Boeing 727.

Several design concepts of a stretched 727, designated the 727-300, emerged between 1970 and 1975. The concept aircraft that began to gain some interest from the airlines, especially United Airlines, was the 727-300B. The proposed aircraft was almost 18ft 4in (5.6m) longer than the 727-200 and included 55 additional seats, new engines (Pratt & Whitney JT8D-217), a larger, high-lift wing (wing span increased by 5ft; 1.5m) with Boeing 747-style outer leading-edge Krueger flaps, inboard slats and double-slotted (as opposed to triple slotted) trailing edge flaps, an increase in the tail plane span by 3ft 4in (1m) and new, four-wheel, main landing gear. Test data suggested that the 727-300B could save around 14% in fuel costs per seat compared with the 727-200. Boeing believed that United Airlines would be their launch customer for the 727-300B, but in August 1975 the airline chose to not order the aircraft. The savings on fuel burn were considered insufficient to compensate for the increased cost of purchasing the airliner. With fuel prices rising and increasing public concern about jet engine noise, the carrier was looking for a more fuel-efficient and quieter aircraft. As a result, Boeing went back to the drawing board and decided to only consider design concepts that included a new wing and wing-mounted, high by-pass ratio engines in an attempt to satisfy customer requirements for lower costs and increased fuel efficiency. The new aircraft concepts were designated 7N7.

CHAPTER 1: ORIGIN, DESIGN AND DEVELOPMENT OF THE 757

In 1976, Boeing released details of its first design attempts for the 7N7 aircraft. It was a narrow bodied airliner featuring a new, advanced technology wing and two wing-mounted General Electric/SNECMA CFM56 or Pratt &Whitney JT10D engines, both of which were in development. The aircraft fuselage and horizontal and vertical stabilisers had a 40-50% commonality with the Boeing 737, with the forward body, cockpit and nose structure of the 727/737. Three different versions (761-119, 761-120 and 761-143) were proposed of varying fuselage length, accommodating between 120 and 180 passengers, with a range capability from 1,300 to over 1,800 nautical miles. The design concepts were very much a derivative of the 737, and closely resembled the Boeing 737 Next Generation family which were launched in 1993.

By mid-1977 the 7N7 had evolved into a largely new design concept with a wider fuselage (by 6 inches), wing-mounted engines and the re-emergence of a horizontal stabiliser adopting a T-tail arrangement. The basis for the proposals had moved away from the 737 and back towards a derivative of the 727. In response to feedback from airlines, including British Airways and Eastern Air Lines, the passenger capacity was established as 160-180 seats. Towards the end of 1977, in response to a request from United Airlines for an increase in cabin width to improve customer comfort, a new iteration emerged where the traditional six-abreast cabin was replaced by seven-abreast seating in a two-aisle configuration. However, there were concerns within Boeing that the design and size of the 7N7 had come too close to the 7X7 and would potentially challenge it in the market place. Also the seven-abreast configuration was unpopular with the airlines as it meant that only one row of seats was added at the expense of an additional aisle. A further complication was the inability of the fuselage cross-

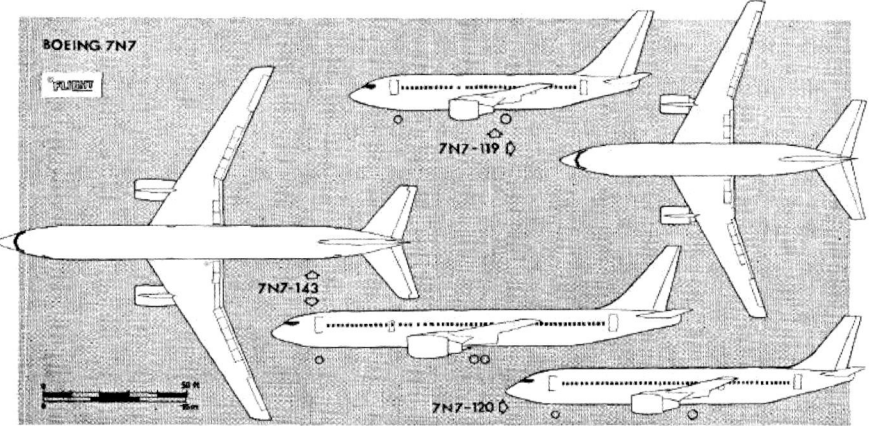

Boeing 7N7 concept aircraft 761-119, 761-120 and 761-143. (Author's collection)

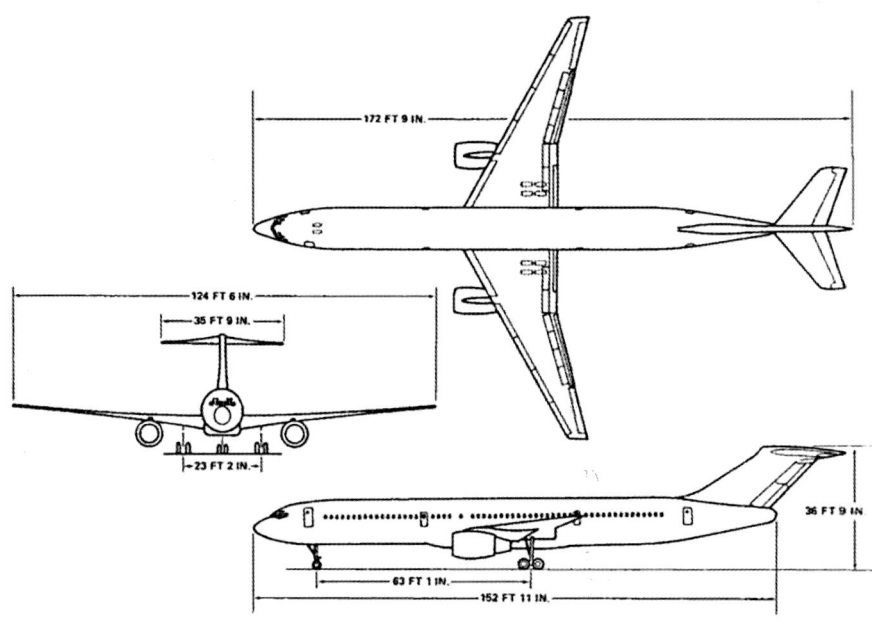

Line diagrams of a mid-1978 version of the 7N7. The wingspan has increased from 114ft 11in to 124ft 6in, almost the final span, while the wing sweep remains 25 degrees. (Author's collection)

An early 1978 concept of the 7N7 with t-tail (Author's collection)

Wind tunnel tests of a 757 concept model. (Boeing)

section to accommodate two standard LD3 cargo containers in the under-floor hold.

In early 1978 the 7N7 returned to a narrow-body design with a six-abreast, single aisle configuration, based on the fuselage cross-section of the Boeing 727, and a two-crew flight deck. It had a new wing with a span of 114ft 11in and a 25 degrees sweep angle, a main landing gear with two wheels per unit, and two wing-mounted high-bypass engines, for which the options included the General Electric CF6-32, Rolls-Royce RB.211-535 or the Pratt &Whitney JT8D-209 or JT10D. The seating capacity was 150-170 and the range was projected to be 1,650 nautical miles (nm).

The two main potential customers for the Boeing 757, Eastern Air Lines and British Airways, had a significant input in the final design of the aircraft, although their requirements differed. British Airways wanted each of the main landing gear units to have two wheels to reduce the weight of the aircraft but had to eventually compromise on the four wheel units requested by Eastern. An initial stretch to accommodate two additional seat rows in order to meet Eastern's 162 seat requirement was followed by a further fuselage stretch to create sufficient space for another three rows of seats, bringing the capacity to 180 (two-class configuration) in order to fulfil British Airways' plans to accommodate around 190 passengers in a high density single class configuration. This model was eventually designated the 757-200.

A shorter variant, designated the 757-100, which could accommodate 160 passengers, was another option but received very little interest from airlines and was never built.

The 757 was officially launched in August 1978 with the announcement of orders for forty aircraft from British Airways (19 aircraft) and Eastern Airlines (21 aircraft), both favouring the Rolls-Royce RB211-535 engine. When the orders were placed the 757 still had a strong resemblance to the Boeing 727, including a T-tail and the same nose section. However, subsequent modifications resulted in the design progressively departing from a derivative of the 727 and 737, and the 757 emerged as entirely new aircraft in its own right.

By February 1979 the T-tail layout had been replaced by a conventional fuselage-mounted low-tail configuration which improved the stability of the aircraft, eliminating potential deep-stall problems associated with T-tail aircraft and ensuring commonality with the Boeing 767 programme. The change to a low tail also allowed the length of the aircraft to be decreased from 172ft 9in to 155ft 3in while the cabin capacity remained unchanged.

The other major external change resulted from the adoption of the newly designed, advanced technology 767 flight deck, which involved grafting the wider and more rounded nose section and cockpit structure of the 767 onto the narrow-body fuselage of the 757. The cockpit had to be installed several inches below the cabin floor level, creating a distinctive blunter, rounded nose which appeared to droop slightly, the mid-point of the nose being below the centreline of the fuselage. However, it afforded greater flight deck visibility and a more spacious working area for the crew.

Another difference between the 757-200 and the 727 was the use of new lighter structural materials, such as aluminium alloys, advanced graphite composites and Kevlar in the construction of parts of the 757-200 airframe which resulted in a significant reduction in the weight of the aircraft.

With the 757 and 767 designs emerging more or less at the same time, their parallel development ended up with the aircraft having a high degree of

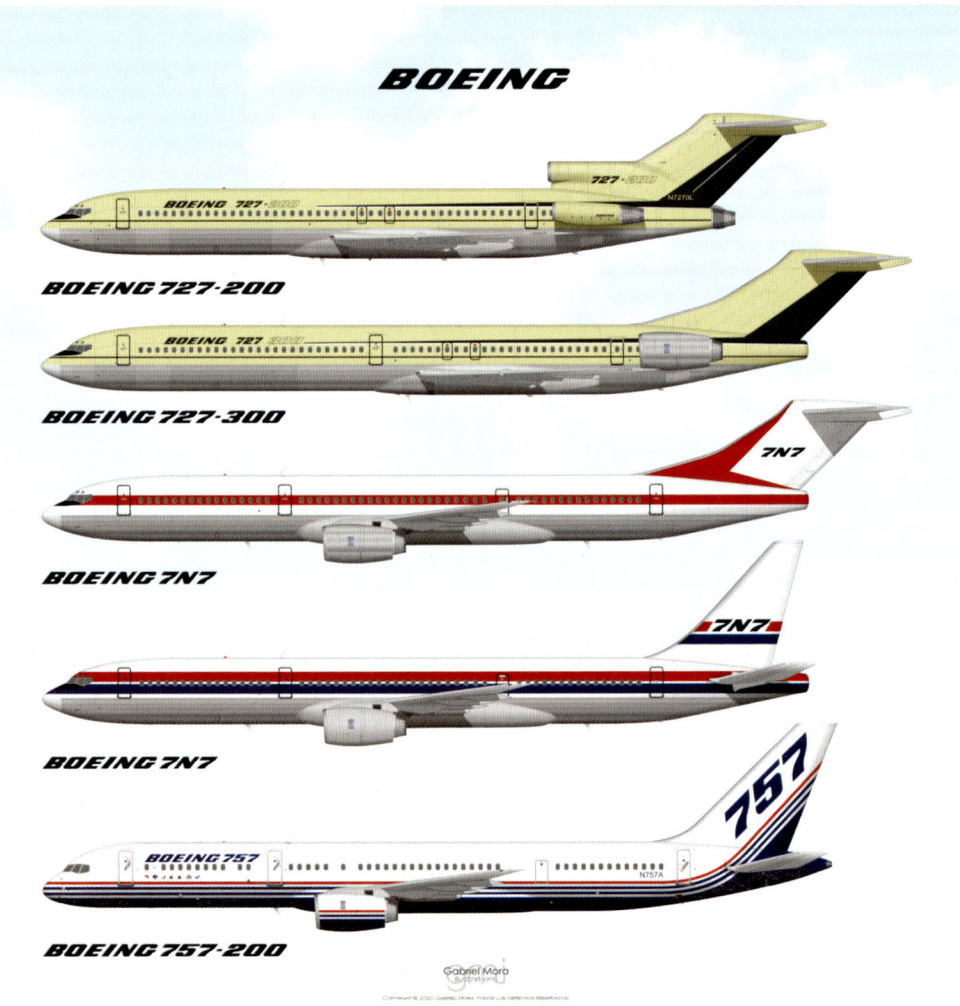

Summary diagram showing some of the stages in the design of the Boeing 757. Note the Boeing 727-300 depicted here is twin-engined, with the centre engine removed on this concept variant. (Gabriel Mora Aldama)

Roll-out of the 757-200 prototype, N757A, at Renton on 13 January 1982. (Boeing)

The Boeing 757-200 prototype following its first emergence from the factory at Renton in January 1982. (Boeing)

commonality, including the same engines, build materials, aerodynamics, components, systems and an almost identical two-pilot cockpit, with fully computerised avionics and high-definition, electronic flight instrumentation system displays. It resulted in a common type rating for pilots to fly both aircraft.

The final approval for production of the 757-200 was announced on 23 March 1979 and the construction of components for the first aircraft began at Boeing's Renton site in Washington in December 1979. Major assembly started at Renton in January 1981 and was completed by September. The Boeing 757-200 prototype (N757A) was rolled out of the factory on 13 January 1982. The lower fuselage was painted blue and the upper fuselage white, with patriotic red, white and blue stripes running along the length of the fuselage and curving up the vertical stabiliser. The engines were painted in a similar scheme to the fuselage. BOEING 757 was painted in blue on the upper fuselage and 757 on the vertical stabiliser.

The maiden flight of the 757 prototype from Renton was on 19 February 1982. The aircraft was powered by Rolls-Royce RB.211-535C engines. The duration of the flight was 2hr 31min before the aircraft landed at the Boeing Flight Test Centre, Boeing Field near Seattle. An intensive flight test programme followed. The early stages of the programme focused on aerodynamics and aircraft handling and manoeuvrability at both low and high speeds. During the next five months the test fleet increased, with the addition of N501EA, the first production aircraft for Eastern Airlines, on 28 March 1982, then N502EA on 29 April, N503EA on 4 June and N504EA on 2 July 1982.

All five aircraft in the test fleet were used for various phases of development testing with the aim of obtaining Federal Aviation Administration (FAA) certification by December 1982. The scope of the test flying included flight systems, engine performance, low speed stability, cruise performance, landing and take-off performance, rejected take-off braking, hot and cold weather trials and route-proving flights. Much of the testing included a focus on the new-technology cockpit and the associated avionics.

A static test programme was also completed as part of the certification process. This involved using an airframe in a test rig to simulate multiple flight cycles by subjecting it to increasing loads using hydraulic jacks. The structural testing simulated 100,000 flights and 40 years of operation. The data obtained provided precise information on the aircraft's structural capability and were used to identify potential areas of inadequate strength and metal fatigue. After a rigorous 14-month test programme, the static tests were completed on 16 July 1982 when the airframe was stressed to destruction to determine the aircraft's absolute strength. After applying excessively high loads on the wings, they both failed at 112% of the load predicted by engineers (i.e. it was 12% stronger than estimated). This allowed the 757's gross weight to be increased from 220,000lb (99,800kg) to 240,000lb (108,900kg).

The first 757-200 for British Airways (G-BIKA) made its maiden flight on 28 October 1982 and subsequently joined the Civil Aviation Authority (CAA) certification programme. The fifth production aircraft (N505EA) completed several sales tours, visiting potential customers in South-East Asia in August 1982 followed by Europe, the Middle East, Africa, and North and South America in the October and November. The latter tour involved 67 flights covering 46,600nm, all without any significant mechanical problems. The tours provided valuable data on operational reliability for the certification process.

The prototype 757, N757A, in flight. (Boeing)

The 757 prototype N757A landing at Boeing Field near Seattle. (Gerry Barron)

The first production 757, N501EA, which was used in the test and certification programme until delivery to Eastern Air Lines in August 1983. (Martin Oertle)

The fourth production 757 to be built, N504EA, was initially used in the test and certification programme before delivery to Eastern Air Lines in February 1983. (LRS747)

The flight test programme involved 1,380 hours of flight. Some of the outcomes showed that the 757 had performed better than expected. For example, the design estimates had predicted a 12% improvement in wing efficiency but in reality it (efficiency of the wing) was almost 17% better than that of the Boeing 727. Savings on fuel-burn were 3.1-4.6% better than engineer predictions. The RB.211-powered 757 received FAA certification on 21 December 1982 followed by CAA certification on 14 January 1983.

Production

The start of production of the 757 coincided with the gradual reduction of the 727 programme. Boeing established a purpose-built assembly line at Renton alongside the 737 production line. It comprised six assembly stages. An individual aircraft moved from station to station where each assembly stage was completed. The initial stages involved: (1) attachment of each wing to the mid-fuselage section; (2) joining of the rear or aft fuselage section (without the horizontal and vertical stabilisers) to the mid-fuselage section; (3) joining of the forward fuselage section (including the nose section with the flight deck equipment installed) with the mid-fuselage section; (4) attachment of the horizontal and vertical stabilisers to the airframe; (5) installation of the electrical and hydraulic systems, flaps and slats and cockpit panels; and (6) fitting of the landing gear. At this point the aircraft was ready for final assembly.

Various stages of the final assembly included installation of the galleys and toilets, testing of the hydraulic and electrical systems, attachment of the engines and fitting of the carpets and seats. The aircraft were usually painted at Renton before being flown to Boeing Field for production testing and

The fifth production aircraft, N505EA, completed several sales tours to South-East Asia, Europe, the Middle East, Africa and North and South America before being delivered to Eastern Air Lines in May 1983. ('N505EA' by wiltshirespotter, licensed under CC BY-SA 2.0)

Boeing 757-200 G-BIKA made its maiden flight on 28 October 1982 and subsequently joined the Civil Aviation Authority's (CAA) 757 certification programme. It was delivered to British Airways at the end of March 1983. ('British Airways Boeing 757-236; G-BIKA@ZRH;22.03.1998' by Aero Icarus, licensed under CC BY-SA 2.0)

Final assembly of the Boeing 757-200 at Renton, Washington, U.S.A. (Boeing)

Boeing 757-300 N757X takes off on the maiden flight of the -300 variant on 2 August 1998. (Boeing)

customer acceptance.

Major components for the aircraft were manufactured at locations away from the Renton assembly line. Boeing produced over 50% of the parts for the aircraft, including the fuselage sections and the wings, with the Military Aircraft Division responsible for the nose and cockpit sections; the fixed leading edges of the wings being produced by the Vertol Division. The remaining components were supplied by a number of predominantly US-based subcontractors. For example, Vought Aircraft produced the horizontal and vertical stabilisers, Goodrich supplied the leading-edge slats and Northrop Grumman manufactured the spoilers. Outside of the US, Short Brothers of Northern Ireland supplied the inboard wing trailing-edge flaps, CASA of Spain produced the outboard wing trailing-edge flaps and Hawker de Havilland of Australia provided the wing in-spar ribs.

Boeing 757-300

At the Farnborough Air Show in 1996, Boeing announced the stretched 757-300, the first major development of the 757 since its initial launch in 1978. The aircraft was mainly aimed at European charter airlines operating inclusive tour holiday flights which enabled them to carry more passengers at lower costs. One such carrier was the German charter company, Condor. It required a low-cost, high-capacity aircraft to replace its ageing McDonnell Douglas DC-10s and saw the longer 757 as the answer. After lengthy discussions with Boeing, Condor placed an order for twelve aircraft with options for an additional twelve and was to be the launch customer of the 757-300.

The longer, stretched 757-300 involved an extension of the front fuselage section by 13ft 4in (4.06m) and a

10ft (3.05m) extension of the rear fuselage section. This would provide accommodation for between 243 and 289 passengers depending on the seating configuration. Although the aircraft retained the same wings as the 757-200, it had to be structurally reinforced to accommodate the increased weights and the additional load that the extended fuselage posed. The wing and centre fuselage section were strengthened together with an increase in the thickness of the skin of the front and rear fuselage sections. The horizontal stabiliser and the undercarriage were also strengthened. New wheels on the landing gear were fitted with 26-ply tyres to deal with the heavier landing weights and predicted higher touchdown speeds. A retractable tail-skid was fitted to prevent possible damage to the rear fuselage as a result of tail strikes during take-off and landing. In addition, an associated body-contact sensor was installed which alerted the flight crew to a potentially more serious contact with the ground on rotation during take-off. Further protection was provided by an upgrade to the spoiler deployment system so that if the nose is too high or the speed too slow during landing the spoiler deployment is delayed, bringing the nose down and reducing the chances of a tail strike.

The first 757-300 (N757X) was rolled out at the Renton factory on 31 May 1998, painted in a red, white and blue livery. It made its 2hr 25min maiden flight on 2 August 1998. Three aircraft were used in the flight test programme, all of which were production aircraft that were eventually delivered to Condor. Test flying involving N757X, the workhorse of the test fleet, included evaluation of the aircraft's structures and systems, control and stability characteristics, rejected take-offs, autoland trials and assessment of the retractable tail skid.

The first 757-300 was initially registered by Boeing as N757X for flight test purposes, before delivery to Condor as D-ABOA in June 1999. It is shown here operating for Condor in 2004. (Javier Rodriguez)

The second 757-300 to join the flight test programme in September 1998 was initially registered as N6067B and painted in the Condor livery. (Dan Stijovich)

Another view of 757-300 N6067B returning to the March Air Reserve Base, California, U.S.A. following a test flight. (Dan Stijovich)

A third 757-300, N1787B, joined the test fleet at the beginning of October 1998, again painted in the Condor livery. It was delivered to Condor as D-ABOC in May 1999. (LRS747)

The second 757-300, initially registered N6067B and painted in the Condor livery, joined the flight test programme on 4 September 1998. It completed high and low-speed runs through a water trough to establish if a water spray deflector was required to avoid water splash from the nose-wheel entering the engines. The tests showed that a deflector was not required. Other tasks included testing of the autoland system in severe wind conditions and lengthy flights to determine the fuel consumption of the Rolls-Royce RB.211-535-powered aircraft.

The third 757-300 (N1787B) joined the test fleet at the beginning of October, again painted in the Condor livery. This aircraft was initially used for testing the attenuation effect of the fuselage on high energy radiation fields (HERF). It went on to be used in tests of smoke penetration, detection and suppression in the cabin and cargo compartments, before completing a four day, service-ready demonstration tour from Frankfurt to eleven of Condor's popular holiday destinations, including the Balearic Islands and the Canaries.

After completing 1,286 hours of ground testing and 912 flying hours, involving more than 356 test flights, the 757-300 received FAA certification in January 1999 together with 180 minute extended range twin-engine operations (ETOPS) approval and the European Joint Aviation Authorities (JAA) type certification.

Assembly of the 757-300s was completed at Renton, on the same production line as the 757-200 aircraft.

Chapter 2:

The 757 Described

Fuselage

The fuselage of the 757-200 is 155ft 3in long (47.32m), with a height of 44ft 6in (13.56m) and a width of 12ft 4in (3.76m). The width is the same as the Boeing 707, 727 and 737. The interior cabin has a length of 118ft 4in (36.09m) and width of 11ft 7in (3.53m).

The 757-300 has a fuselage length of 178ft 7in (54.5m), 23ft 4in longer than the 757-200, and a cabin length of 141ft 7in (43.15m). All other dimensions are identical to the 757-200.

Use of Composite Materials

Lighter and stronger composite materials have been used to construct the 757 airframe compared to other earlier Boeing models, which contribute to significant weight savings and improved fuel efficiency. Carbon fibre advanced graphite is used for primary moveable surfaces such as ailerons, elevators, spoilers, flaps and the rudder, as well as the engine cowls. Carbon-reinforced aramid composites (Kevlar-reinforced plastic) are used for secondary fairing structures including the nose and main landing gear doors, the fixed training edge panels on the wings, engine pylon fairings and the wing to fuselage fairings.

Improved aluminium alloys used in the manufacture of the wings provide a significant reduction in the weight of the wing structure, greater toughness, increased strength and improved corrosion and fatigue resistance.

Titanium alloys are used in the support structure for the main landing gear, various fuselage fittings, including high pressure tubing and ducting, and for firewalls and door thresholds.

Carbon brakes are used instead of traditional steel units on the 757-300 and as an option on the 757-200, providing higher energy absorption capability, longer service life as well as contributing to a reduction in the weight of the aircraft.

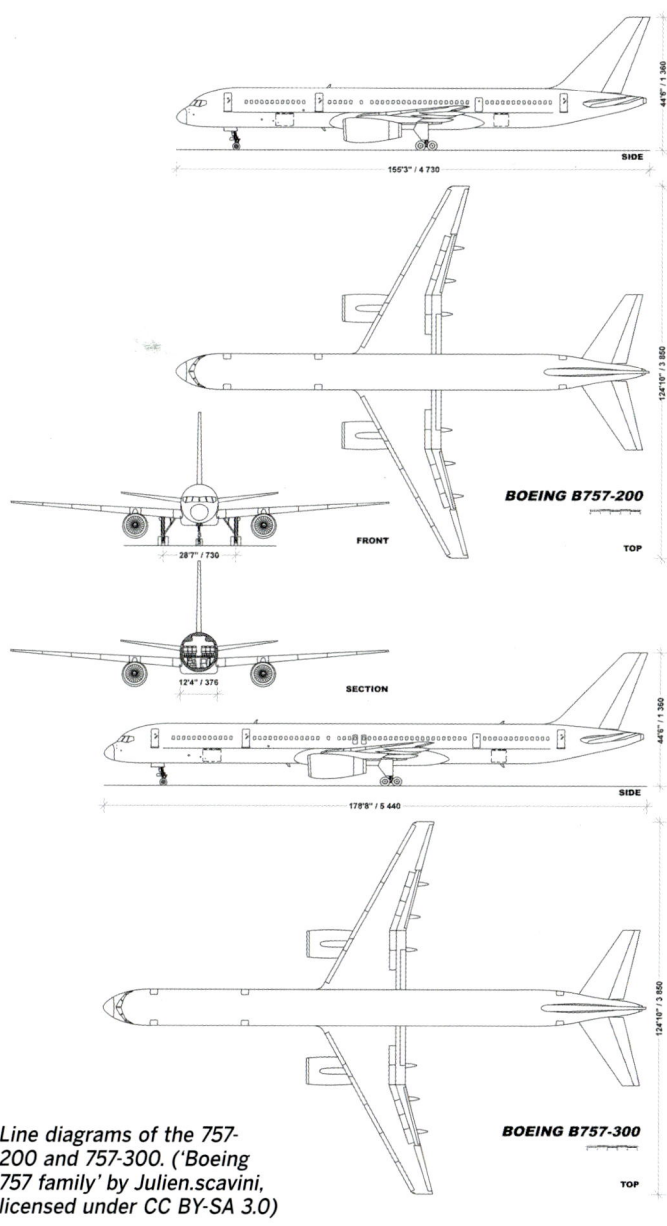

Line diagrams of the 757-200 and 757-300. ('Boeing 757 family' by Julien.scavini, licensed under CC BY-SA 3.0)

Wings

The 757 features an advanced-technology wing design. The wing has a sharp leading edge, relatively flat top and a small under-wing cusp near the trailing edge, using what is referred to as an aft-loaded design technology. This shape produces lift across more of the upper surface of the wing as opposed to a narrow area close behind the leading edge and has less aerodynamic drag. Owing to the aircraft's relatively low average speed, a reduced wing sweep of 25 degrees can be used without too much concern about drag. Reduced drag also improves fuel efficiency. In addition, the wings are more than 20% thicker than those of the 757's predecessor, the Boeing 727, creating more lift, a substantial reduction in drag and greater fuel storage capacity, resulting in increased range. The thicker wing also allows an increase in the wingspan, producing less lift-induced drag.

The wings are optimised for a cruising speed of Mach 0.8 as the 757 was designed specifically for economical operation of short-haul routes, where time spent climbing and descending almost equals the time spent cruising, so speed is less important.

The wings are largely identical across all variants of the 757. The span is 124ft 10in (38.0m), leading to a wing area of 1,994 sq ft (185.25 sq m). The main structure of the wing is constructed from aluminium alloys. The wings provide storage for fuel, accommodate fuel-system equipment, support the engines and contain the aircraft's main control surfaces, including flaps, ailerons, slats and spoilers. The wide junction between the wing and the fuselage (the wing root) allows ample space for storage of the retracted main landing gear.

In the late 1990s blended winglets, initially developed to reduce the impact of induced drag on the circulation of air around the wing of the Boeing 737NG Series, were approved for the 757. Many 757-200s, in particular those belonging to US carriers including American Airlines, Delta Airlines and United Airlines, were retrofitted with the winglets and designated 757-200W or 757-200WL. The winglets contributed to improved fuel efficiency and extended the range of the aircraft from 3,915nm to 4,100nm.

A Scimitar Blended Winglet was introduced to the 757-200 in 2016. It used the existing blended winglet technology, replacing the aluminium tip caps with sharply swept back scimitar tips and adding a small outboard aerodynamic trailing edge wedge to the lower part of the winglet. The modification reduced fuel burn by a further 1.1% over the blended winglets and by more than 6%

CHAPTER 2: THE 757 DESCRIBED

when compared with a 757 without winglets. United Airlines and Icelandair were the first carriers to install and operate scimitar blended winglets on their 757-200 aircraft.

The wing houses a number of high-lift devices which serve to increase wing lift and decrease stall speed during take-off, approach and landing. These include flaps on the trailing edge of the wing and slats on the leading edge. All the flaps are double-slotted except for the outer section of each inboard flap, adjacent to the engine, which is single slotted to avoid interruption with the jet wake. The slats run along the full span of the wing and are in five sections composed of a large, single inboard slat and four outboard slats. The extension of the trailing edge flaps during take-off and landing leads to the deployment of the leading edge slats. The combination increases the effective wing area and the curvature (camber) of the wing and, hence, increases the lift generated by the wing.

There are two inboard (in front of the inboard flap) and four outboard (in front of the outboard flap) spoilers on the upper surface of each wing. Ten spoilers (flight spoilers) open together for use as speed brakes or partially extend on one wing to bank the aircraft, supplementing the ailerons. The two innermost spoilers (ground spoilers) are only used on the ground to dump lift. On the ground, the ten flight spoilers also extend and function as ground speed brakes.

A scimitar blended winglet on an Icelandair 757-200. (Icelandair)

Underside view of Boeing 757 NZ7572 of the Royal New Zealand Air Force showing the wing shape and form. (Pseudopanax)

A blended winglet on a Jet2.com 757. (Author's collection)

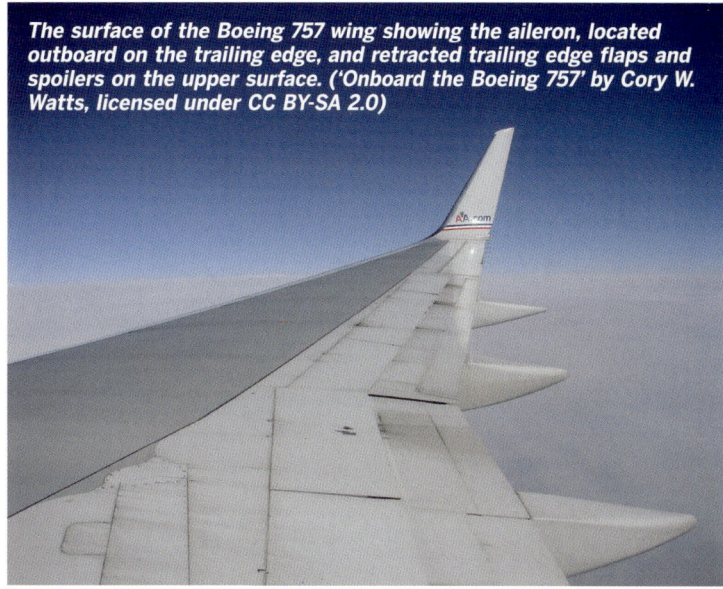

The surface of the Boeing 757 wing showing the aileron, located outboard on the trailing edge, and retracted trailing edge flaps and spoilers on the upper surface. ('Onboard the Boeing 757' by Cory W. Watts, licensed under CC BY-SA 2.0)

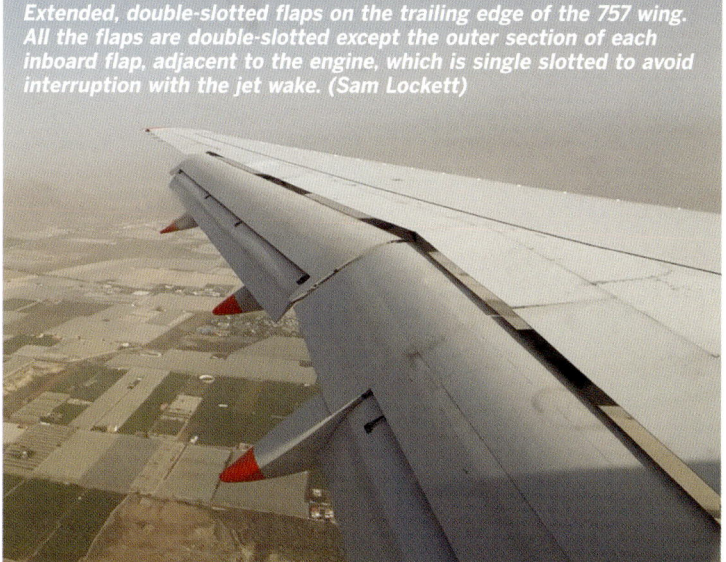

Extended, double-slotted flaps on the trailing edge of the 757 wing. All the flaps are double-slotted except the outer section of each inboard flap, adjacent to the engine, which is single slotted to avoid interruption with the jet wake. (Sam Lockett)

The extended double-slotted and single-slotted trailing edge flaps of the Boeing 757 are clearly visible on this underside image of former First Choice 757, G-OOBC. (Adrian Pingstone)

A Jet2.com 757-236 landing at Manchester Airport with the extended, four outboard slats clearly visible on the leading edge of the wing. (Author's collection)

The extended spoilers on the upper surface of the 757 wing acting as ground speed brakes. (Sam Lockett)

The rear fuselage and tail of a Jet2.com Boeing 757-236. (Author's collection)

The flaps and slats are normally mechanically controlled and powered by the hydraulic system. An alternate system (used when there is a problem with the primary control/operating system) allows direct manual operation of the flaps and slats through electric motors. The spoilers are powered by the hydraulic system and commanded by a basic fly-by-wire system, which uses electrical signalling instead of control cables.

Primary Flight Controls

The 757 has two, relatively long span ailerons for roll control, located outboard of the trailing edge flaps. They operate in conjunction with the flight spoilers.

The horizontal stabilisers or tail are moved to maintain the aircraft in longitudinal trim and static stability. Elevators for pitch control are located on the trailing edge of the horizontal stabilisers.

The fixed vertical stabiliser or tail fin has a movable rudder hinged to the trailing edge for yaw control. The rudder is primarily used during take-off and landing to maintain runway centreline alignment, especially during strong cross-winds, and to compensate for the yaw effect of asymmetric thrust from the wing-mounted engines due to engine problems or an engine failure.

The primary flight controls are powered by the hydraulic system.

The left horizontal stabiliser of a 757-200 with the elevator on the trailing edge deflected downwards. (Ahmed Orgunwall/Airlinercafe.com)

Hydraulic System

The Boeing 757 has three independent hydraulic systems: centre, left and right systems. The system reservoirs are pressurised using bleed air from either the engine or the auxiliary power unit. The distribution system consists of titanium pipes.

The centre hydraulic system is dedicated to the primary flight controls, although these can be powered by any of the three systems. The main components of the centre hydraulic system include a reservoir for hydraulic fluid, two separately-powered electric motor-driven pumps and a ram air turbine. The system is powered by the electric motor pumps, however, should both engines fail leading to a loss of normal electrical power, sufficient hydraulic power for adequate aircraft control by the centre system can be provided by the ram air turbine. This is located in the body fairing behind the right wing landing gear.

Landing gear extension and retraction, nose wheel steering, flaps and slats, left engine thrust reverser and the alternate brake system are primarily powered by the left hydraulic system. The left hydraulic system consists of a reservoir, an engine-driven pump (the main pump) and an electric motor-driven pump to provide additional hydraulic power. If the left system becomes inoperable, it can be powered by the right hydraulic system through a power transfer unit, using the residual hydraulic fluid from the left system.

The components and operation of the right hydraulic system is similar to the left system. It powers the normal and reserve brake systems, and the right engine thrust reverser.

Electrical System

The electrical system generates, transmits and distributes both alternating current (AC) and direct current (DC) power throughout the aircraft to power the aircraft systems. In the 757 it comprises the main AC and DC power systems, a battery and standby power system and a hydraulic-driven generator system. The 757 has left- and right-hand side electrical systems, which are normally powered by the left- and right-hand engines respectively. Therefore, each system is essentially independent from the other.

The main source of the aircraft's electrical power is the AC system. The entire AC electrical requirement of the aircraft can be supplied by any two of the main AC sources which are the left and right engine generators and the Auxiliary Power Unit (APU) generator. Power from each engine generator is routed to a respective left and right main AC bus, from where it is transferred to the equipment drawing on it. If an engine generator fails, the remaining one can power the bus of the failed generator. The APU generator, which connects to both main AC busses, can be used to provide power if one or both engine generators stop operating or on the ground when the engines are turned off. AC power can also be supplied by an external power unit when on the ground.

The 757 has a triplex autoland system; three separate autopilots are powered by different sources for safety. Therefore, in addition to the left and right main systems, a smaller centre AC bus is provided which routes power from the battery-standby system to the autopilot.

CHAPTER 2: THE 757 DESCRIBED

The hydraulic-driven generator system operates automatically when both the left- and right-hand main AC busses have no power. It is powered by the aircraft's left-hand side hydraulic system and supplies power to the left, right and standby AC busses, the captain's flight instruments and DC power to the battery and standby DC busses. However, only a small amount of DC power is produced by the hydraulic-driven generator.

The main DC electrical system uses two transformer rectifiers (part of the left and right electrical systems) which convert AC power to DC current. The transformer rectifiers are powered from the respective left and right main AC busses and normally operate independently from one another.

In the event of failure of the main AC and DC systems, the battery and standby system can supply both AC and DC power to selected flight instruments and the navigation and communication systems. There are two batteries on a 757 that can supply power for the standby power system. The system should be able to provide sufficient electrical power for up to 90 minutes.

Fuel System

The 757's fuel system consists of three integral sealed tanks: left and right outer tanks, located in the wings, mostly outboard of the engines, which each have a capacity of 8,237 litres, and a centre section tank (capacity: 26,123 litres) located between the spars of the wing carry-through section, which runs under the cabin floor from and between the inboard sections of the wings. There are surge tanks at each wing tip for fuel overflow which drains back to the centre tank.

Fuel is supplied to each of the three tanks through dual fuel nozzle adapters at the fuelling point/station located under the right wing, outboard of the engine. Each tank has two AC-powered fuel pumps that ensure fuel flow to the engines. The centre tank fuel is used first and, when this is empty, each engine is supplied from its respective wing tank. Fuel can be transferred between the left and right tanks to ensure a balanced fuel load is maintained, especially during single-engine operations.

The steerable nose-wheel unit of the 757. ('G-BIKB Boeing 757-236 British Airways' by aceebee, licensed under CC BY-SA 2.0)

Undercarriage

The two main undercarriage units have four wheels in tandem pairs. The undercarriage legs are mounted on the lower inner wing and retract sideways for storage in the wing root. A landing gear door opens to allow the wheels to retract into the wheel well, and then closes. The nose undercarriage consists of a steerable twin wheel unit which retracts forward.

Undercarriage extension, retraction and nose-wheel steering is powered by the left hydraulic system. In an emergency it is possible to lower the undercarriage by gravity.

Each main undercarriage wheel has multiple disc steel or carbon brakes, in contrast to the nose wheels which have no brakes. The normal brake system is powered by the right hydraulic system but, if there are problems of low hydraulic pressure on the right side system, an alternate brake system comes into operation powered by the left hydraulic system. If a situation arises where both the right and left hydraulic systems are compromised, the reserve brake system provides power for the brakes. Reserve hydraulic fluid is supplied to the right hydraulic system electric motor-driven pump, which is isolated from the other right system components and provides pressure to the normal brake system. The braking systems have antiskid protection.

Flight Deck and Cockpit Systems

The 757 has a two crew cockpit with an additional jump seat for an observer. The flight deck has fully integrated electronic systems including:

1. Flight Management System (FMS)
2. Electronic Flight Instrument System (EFIS)
3. Automatic Flight Control System (AFCS)
4. Engine Indication and Crew Alerting System (EICAS)

Eight cathode-ray tube (CRT) screens display information from the systems to the flight crew. A number of airlines have retrofitted several of the CRT displays with a flat panel LCD display system. More recently, Rockwell Collins and Boeing have offered an upgrade which involves replacing six of the cathode-ray tube displays with large format LCD screens. The large format display system provides more information to pilots.

The Flight Management System, through the Flight Management Computer System, assists the flight crew with flight planning, including navigation, in-flight performance optimisation for best economy and

The port wing root, fairing, engine, and main undercarriage unit of an American Airlines 757-200. ('American Airlines 757-200 Port wing root, fairing, engine, main gear' by Bill Abbott, licensed under CC BY-SA 2.0)

automatic fuel monitoring. Route and flight plan data is entered into the flight management computer through a control display unit. The computer uses this data together with the navigation database and aircraft systems data to calculate the pitch, roll and engine thrust setting commands for manual and automatic flight path guidance for all phases of the flight, from immediately after take-off, to cruise and approach and landing. It can predict the optimum flight profile and flight path, including altitudes and speeds which will be the most fuel-efficient and/or of shortest duration. The control commands are sent to the autopilot flight director system and the auto-throttle system. The flight map and route data is sent to the Horizontal Situation Indicator for display. The flight management computer is controlled through two control display units which are located either side of the forward section of the central console between the pilots. The original 757 avionics were replaced by a new Honeywell Pegasus flight management computer in 1999, in conjunction with the introduction of the 757-300. Other additions included an enhanced ground proximity warning system, a predictive windshear system and a global positioning system for navigation during most phases of flight.

The electronic flight instrument system obtains data from various aircraft systems and presents it on two colour cathode ray tube or LCD displays located in front of each pilot: the Attitude Director Indicator (ADI) and the Horizontal Situation Indicator (HSI).

Sources of data include the aircraft's air data inertial reference system for information on the current status and navigation of the aircraft and the flight control and flight management computers and the auto-throttle for data relating to automatic flight.

The original cockpit layout of Northwest Airlines 757-200 N577NW ('The Flight Deck of The Boeing 757' by Cory W. Watts, licensed under CC BY-SA 2.0)

The upgraded flight deck of a Jet2.com Boeing 757-236. (Jet2.com)

The air data inertial reference system comprises three air data inertial reference units (left, right and centre ADIRUs) which combine the inertial reference units and air data computers. Each ADIRU receives navigation data and air data from various sources and processes it for display and use by the aircraft's systems. Data sources include:

- Air data from the aircraft's pitot and static system, obtained through conventional probes and sensors
- Inertial reference system (IRS), which features the first commercial use of ring laser gyroscopes
- Global positioning system (GPS)
- Radio navigation systems, which include automatic direction-finding and distance measuring equipment, two VOR receivers, three instrument landing system (ILS) receivers and the weather radar.

The left and right ADIRUs constantly supply precise air data (airspeed, altitude, angle of attack) and inertial reference navigational information (position, heading, ground speed, attitude) to the flight crew's electronic flight instrument system displays (ADI and HSI).

The ADI is the upper of the two displays (or outer where the two displays are horizontally mounted following a retrofit to a flat panel display) and provides information on the roll and pitch of the aircraft, replacing the old artificial horizon, as well as the ground speed, autopilot status, flight director commands and the localiser/glide slope deviation during an ILS approach.

The lower (or inner) HSI display presents navigational data in several modes: a map mode showing the aircraft's progress along the route on a dynamic map display; a VOR mode showing the aircraft's position relative to selected VORs; an ILS mode used on approach and displaying the aircraft's track in relation to the localiser course and glide slope; and a Plan mode where the aircraft's position and route is presented on a true north up static map display. Traffic, terrain data, weather radar and predicted windshear can also be displayed on the HSI.

The centre ADIRU provides the same air data and navigational information to the aircraft's flight management computer and flight and engine control systems, and may be used as a backup for the left and right ADIRUs.

In the centre of the main instrument panel and visible to both pilots are two Engine Indication and Crew Alerting System (EICAS) colour display units. The upper display is dedicated to primary engine parameters, as well as showing warnings, cautions and advisory information. The lower display shows secondary engine parameters and information on the status of aircraft systems. It can also be used on the ground to retrieve and monitor maintenance information, for verification testing of the major systems and for troubleshooting. The crew alerting system component uses automatic aircraft system monitoring with alert messages shown on the upper display unit. The messages are categorised by priority: warnings, in red, alert the crew to a non-normal operation or system status and require immediate crew attention and corrective action; cautions, in amber; alert the crew to a non-normal operation or system status requiring immediate crew awareness and possible corrective action; advisories, in amber and indented, alert the crew to a non-normal operation or system status requiring routine crew awareness and possible

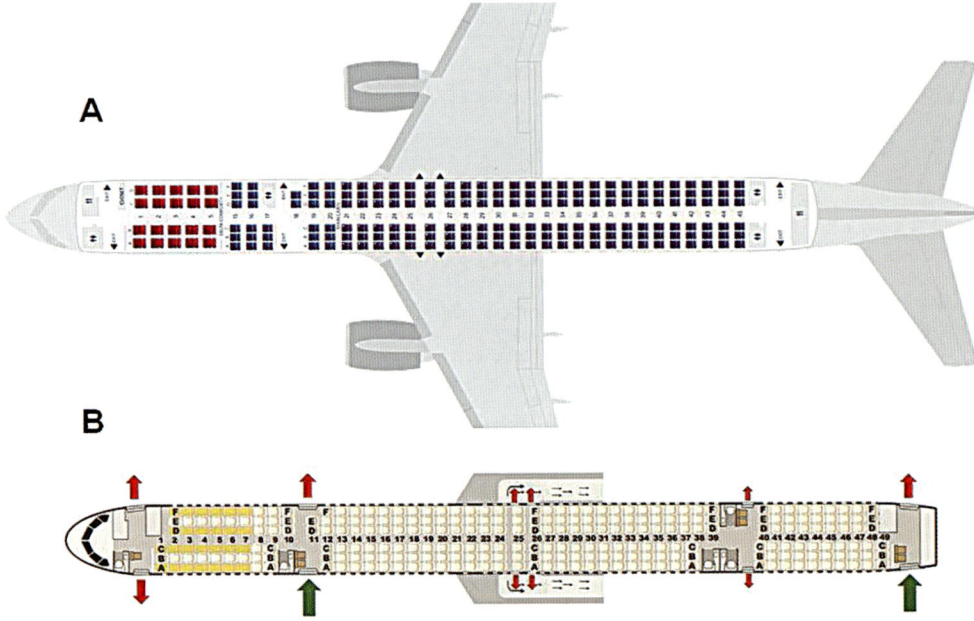

The typical seating configuration of: (A) Delta Air Lines 757-200 and (B) Condor 757-300. (Delta Air Lines; Condor)

corrective action. The EICAS also displays non-system alert messages relating to specific situations including altitude alerts, stall warnings, ground proximity warnings, over-speed warnings, traffic alert and collision avoidance system warnings and windshear warnings.

The 757's automatic flight control system includes the autopilot flight director system (AFDS) and the auto-throttle system. A mode control panel and the flight management computer control the AFDS and the auto-throttle, and direct the aircraft to climb, cruise and descend. The AFDS comprises three flight control computers (FCCs) and the mode control panel. The flight control computers are responsible for the control of hydraulically-powered autopilot servos which operate the ailerons (roll mode) and elevators (pitch mode), with rudder commands only included during a multiple autopilot approach. The autopilot can also control the nose wheel steering following an automatic landing.

The auto-throttle system controls the engine thrust from take-off through to landing. The auto-throttle system is controlled by the thrust management computer using commands from the flight management computer. It can also be overridden through manual inputs from the mode control panel. The thrust management computer uses the auto-throttle function to maintain the commanded airspeed according to the phase of flight and the working temperatures of the engines. The auto-throttle responds to decreases in airspeed by rapid thrust adjustments, whereas when the airspeed is above the command speed, the thrust is slowly reduced.

In addition to the electronic systems and displays, the flight deck also has a range of conventional instruments which assist pilots in flying the aircraft.

Cabin Interior and Seating

The cabin of the 757 features a single centre aisle with up to six seats per row. The interior is designed to give a more spacious appearance, featuring sculptured sidewall and ceiling panels made from carbon fibre composites to save weight, and recessed lighting. The overhead bins are relatively large with approximately $1.9ft^3$ ($0.054m^3$) of space per person. The 757-300 is fitted with a redesigned interior using an architecture and materials originally developed for the Boeing 777 and Next Generation 737. The new, more spacious and user-friendly cabin includes curved ceiling panels with up to 3in of additional headroom, indirect interior lighting, larger and longer overhead bins and an optional continuous handrail which runs along the base of the bins for the entire length of the cabin. The 757-300 interior became an option on all new 757-200s from March 2000.

Recent enhancements to the passenger cabin include lie-flat seats which were introduced by American Airlines in an all-business class cabin before it retired its fleet, new slimline economy seats which were installed by Delta Air Lines, United Airlines and Icelandair, and LED lighting and improved satellite communication entertainment systems, including gate-to-gate wi-fi, which were also introduced by Icelandair.

The front cabin of a Jet2 757-236. (Jet2.com)

A number of interior seating arrangements have been offered for the 757-200 since it first entered into commercial service, typically providing accommodation for 178-239 passengers. The passenger capacity is dependent on the number of cabin doors and emergency exits.

Current two-class seating arrangements for 194 passengers (12 first + 182 economy class) includes three standard cabin doors and a fourth, smaller cabin door just behind the wing on both sides of the aircraft. A second option, which accommodates up to 200 passengers (12 first + 188 economy class), has three standard doors and two over-wing emergency exits on each side of the aircraft. Seating is four-abreast (two-by-two) in first class and six-abreast (three-by three) in the economy class. The egress of passengers from an over-wing emergency exit would normally involve sliding down extended trailing edge flaps. However, the height of the 757 above the ground requires an inflatable slide to be stored in the wing-to-body fairing, just behind the emergency doors. Following opening of the over-wing exits, the ground spoilers are automatically retracted to avoid obstruction and allow the slide to inflate.

For single-class, all economy six-abreast seating, the 757-200 is certified to carry up to 239 passengers in a high density arrangement. In this configuration the aircraft has three standard cabin doors and a fourth, smaller cabin door just behind the wing, together with improved accessibility to the number 2 door in front of the wing.

A three-class seating arrangement option was initially offered by Boeing, involving a four-abreast first class, five-abreast business class and six-abreast economy class.

The longer 757-300 typically carries between 243 passengers (12 first + 231 economy class) in a two-class seating configuration and a certified maximum of 295 passengers in an all economy, single class arrangement. In order to meet FAA regulations, the 757-300 required more exits. This typically includes three standard cabin doors, a smaller cabin door behind the wing, and a pair of over-wing emergency exits on each side of the aircraft.

Engines

The engines for the 757 are supplied by two manufacturers: Rolls-Royce and Pratt & Whitney.

The first engine developed by Roll-Royce was the RB.211-535C, a cropped-fan, three-rotor axial flow powerplant, with a power rating of 37,400lb maximum take-off thrust. It was a derivative of the larger, legacy engine, the RB.211-22B, and a scaled-down version of the more advanced RB.211-524. The smaller size led to an approximately 18% reduction in fan airflow and 12% lower core airflow. The engine was developed to operate at moderate temperatures, pressures and speeds, optimised for short-haul flights and low noise levels.

An improved version of the engine, designated the RB.211-535E4, became available in October 1984, providing an increase in the maximum take-off thrust to 40,200lb and a 3% improvement in fuel consumption. The engine is 16ft 6in (5.03m) long, with a maximum width over the fan casing of 7ft 5in (2.27m) and a height of 7ft 11in (2.41m) from the lowest point of the gearbox to the top of the engine mount pad. Each engine is automatically controlled

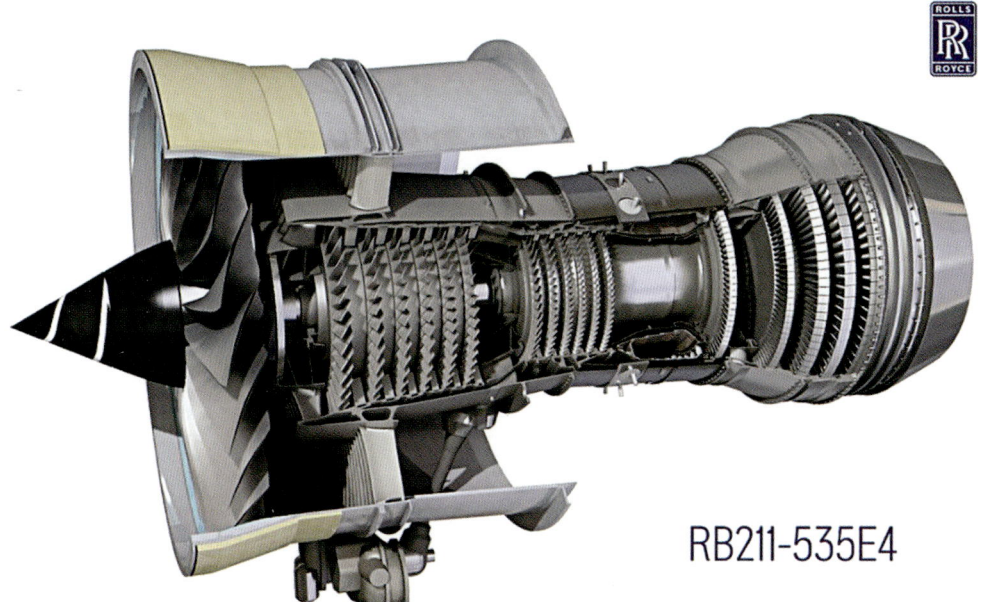

The Rolls-Royce RB211-535E4 engine. (Rolls-Royce)

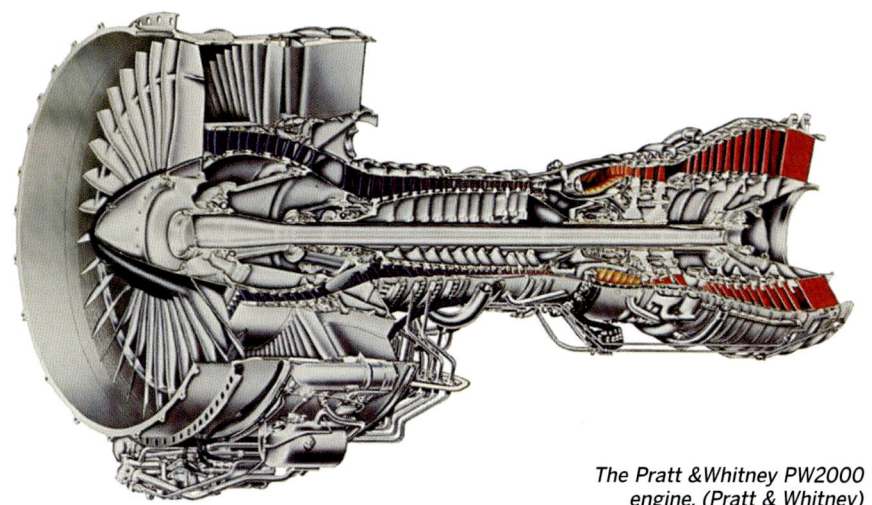

The Pratt & Whitney PW2000 engine. (Pratt & Whitney)

by an electronic engine controller which receives auto-throttle and manual flight crew inputs through the thrust levers. The RB.211-535C could not be modified to the new standard provided by the -535E4, so the improved performance could only be gained through an engine replacement.

The RB.211-535E4 was further up-rated to the RB.211-535E4B by Rolls-Royce, offering an additional 2,000lb of thrust per engine and improved fuel consumption. This engine is used on the 757-300 and is an option for the 757-200.

Pratt & Whitney designed an all-new engine specifically for the 757, the PW2037, a two-rotor axial flow high by-pass turbofan, originally known as the JT10D. Development of the engine started in 1972 with flight testing beginning in February 1983. The engine entered into service on a Delta Airlines' 757 in December 1984. The PW2037 is 12ft 2in (3.73m) in length, and 7ft (2.16m) wide. It is a very fuel-efficient, advanced technology turbofan engine with a take-off thrust range from 37,600 to 43,000lb. The fan diameter of the PW2037 is significantly larger than that of the RB.211-535, which increases the by-pass ratio and results in the extra thrust and 5% improvement in fuel consumption compared with the original RB.211-535C engine. The PW2037 has subsequently been up-rated to the PW2040, followed by the latest standard, designated the PW2043, which provides around 43,850lb of thrust and is used on the 757-300. Previous versions of the PW2000 engine can be converted to the PW2043 standard. In the same way as the RB.211 engine, the PW2037/2040/2043 is controlled by an electric engine controller.

In addition to the main engines, the 757 has a Garrett CTCP 331-200 auxiliary power unit (APU) located in the aircraft's tail cone. The APU is a small gas-turbine engine with an air inlet door between the horizontal and vertical stabilisers on the right hand side of the aircraft. The main purpose of the APU is to supply electrical power on the ground for the aircraft's systems and bleed air for the air conditioning. It can also be started in flight to provide emergency power.

Maintenance of a Rolls-Royce RB211-535 engine on an American Airlines Boeing 757-200. ('starboard engine w/o inlet cowl' by Bill Abbott, licensed under CC BY-SA 2.0)

Chapter 3:
Commercial Passenger Service

Boeing 757 - 200

Eastern Air Lines first two 757-225s (N506EA and N507EA) were delivered in late December 1982. Eastern operated the first 757 commercial service on 1 January 1983, on a flight from the carrier's Atlanta hub to Tampa, Florida. Following its return to Atlanta, the aircraft flew a return trip to Miami.

The first 757 revenue flight by the other launch customer, British Airways, was on 9 February 1983 - a Shuttle service from London Heathrow to Belfast. During the following two months, British Airways gradually introduced the 757 into service on other Shuttle routes to Glasgow, Manchester and Edinburgh, replacing the Hawker Siddeley Trident 3s. A detailed account of British Airways' operation of the Boeing 757-200 is provided in Chapter 4.

The next two carriers to start using the 757 were British charter operators Monarch Airlines and Air Europe. Monarch Airlines placed an order for an initial two 757s in February 1981 and received its first aircraft on 21 March 1983. It entered service five days later, operating inclusive tour charters to European holiday destinations. Air Europe's first 757 was delivered on 6 April 1983 and commenced holiday charter flights seventeen days later.

After the first three months of service, both Eastern Air Lines and British Airways reported a high degree of satisfaction with the 757. The aircraft had demonstrated impressive fuel efficiency and reliability and positive feedback was received from pilots about the flight management systems, navigation, avionics and the electronic display of information.

Delta Air Lines was the second US carrier to introduce the 757-200 into service. Following an order for sixty aircraft placed in November 1980, its first 757 was delivered to Atlanta on 5 November 1984. Delta was the launch customer for the Pratt & Whitney PW2037-powered 757. The inaugural service was on 1 December 1984, from Atlanta to Dayton, Ohio via Birmingham, Alabama.

CHAPTER 3: COMMERCIAL PASSENGER SERVICE

Boeing 757-225 N507EA, the second 757 to be delivered to Eastern Air Lines in late December 1982. (Gerard Helmer)

British Airways took delivery of its first 757-236, G-BIKB, on 25 January 1983. The aircraft was named 'Windsor Castle'. (Danny Grew)

Boeing 757-200 G-MONB was the first aircraft of the type to be acquired by Monarch Airlines in March 1983. ('Monarch Airlines Boeing 757-2T7; G-MONB@ SZG;25.01.2003' by Aero Icarus, licensed under CC BY-SA 2.0)

Air Europe initially placed an order for two 757-200s. Its first example, G-BKRM shown here, was delivered to the operator at London Gatwick Airport on 6 April 1983. ('Air Europe Boeing 757-236; G-BKRM, February 1984' by Aero Icarus, licensed under CC BY-SA 2.0)

Delta Air Lines were the second US operator of the 757. Shown here is 757-232 N607DL, which was delivered to Delta in May 1985. ('Delta Air Lines Boeing 757-232; N607DL@LAS;15.03.2005', by Aero Icarus, licensed under CC BY-SA 2.0)

Northwest Airlines took delivery of its first 757-251 in February 1985. Pictured here at Seattle-Tacoma International Airport is N516US which was delivered to Northwest in July 1986. (LRS747)

Despite their successful introduction into service, the sale of 757s was slow for much of the 1980s. Although the 757 had no direct competitor, lower fuel prices had lessened the emphasis on fuel efficiency, which led to many airlines retaining their fleets of Boeing 727s and Douglas DC-9s. Also post-deregulation changes in the United States resulted in more competition between operators and an emphasis on smaller aircraft. Nevertheless, Northwest Orient Airlines ordered twenty 757s in November 1983, the first aircraft being delivered at the end of February 1985.

By the late 1980s fuel prices had begun to increase, new US airport noise regulations had been introduced and the hub-and-spoke model had led to increased congestion at hub airports in the United States. The larger capacity, fuel-efficient and quieter 757 was the answer to these issues and sales improved dramatically during 1988-89. Around three hundred and twenty-two orders were received, including a combined order of one hundred and sixty from two major US carriers: American Airlines and United Airlines. American Airlines received its first two 757s in July 1989 and by the end of the decade had eight aircraft in service, while United Airlines took delivery of five aircraft during 1989, the first entering service in August of that year.

The 757 was gradually becoming a common feature of high density, short-haul routes and transcontinental services in the United States, replacing the ageing Boeing 707s and 727s, and Douglas DC-8s and DC-9s. The advantages of the 757 became apparent as it began to operate out of airports with size restrictions and strict noise regulations.

In 1986, the FAA approved the Rolls-Royce RB.211-powered 757 for 120 minutes ETOPS (Extended-range

CHAPTER 3: COMMERCIAL PASSENGER SERVICE

American Airlines 757-223 N692AA departing from Los Angeles International Airport. ('N692AA Boeing 757 American Airlines' by aeroprints.com, licensed under CC BY-SA 3.0)

United Airlines received its first five 757s during the second half of 1989. 757-222 N518UA, shown here, was delivered in September 1990. ('United Airlines Boeing 757-222; N518UA@ DCA;19.07.1995' by Aero Icarus, licensed under CC BY-SA 2.0)

Continental Airlines 757-224 N58101 was the first example to be delivered to the carrier in May 1994. Continental built up a fleet of forty-one 757-200s which were transferred to United Airlines in October 2010 following the merger of the two airlines. ('Boeing 757-200, Continental Airlines' by John Taggart, licensed under CC BY-SA 2.0)

Boeing 757-204 N906NV of Allegiant Air, landing at McCarran International Airport, Las Vegas. This aircraft was originally operated by Britannia Airways and Thomson Airways as G-BYAP before it was acquired by Allegiant in April 2012. ('N906NV Allegiant Air 1994 Boeing 757-204 - cn 27236' by Tomás Del Coro, licensed under CC BY-SA 2.0)

Boeing 757-2Q8 N710TW of Trans World Airlines (TWA) at Princess Juliana International Airport, St. Martin in January 1999. ('TWA Boeing 757-2Q8; N710TW@SXM;31.01.1999' by Aero Icarus, licensed under CC BY-SA 2.0)

Boeing 757-23N N204UW was acquired by US Airways from French carrier Air Horizons in February 2006 and initially registered as N643UW. (Author's collection)

Twin-engine Operations Performance Standards) operations. The approval, given by a regulatory body, such as the FAA and CAA, permits twin-engine aircraft to operate in airspace or along a route up to 120 minutes flying time from a suitable diversion airfield at an approved one-engine inoperative cruise speed, over expanses of water or remote land areas. The initial ETOPS flight by a 757 occurred in 1988. Sometime later ETOPS opened up transatlantic route options to the 757 and US and European scheduled airlines began to take up these improved opportunities from May 1990. For US carriers, the lower capacity of the 757 made it highly suited to the thinner transatlantic services from US east coast hubs to secondary European destinations, such as Manchester and Edinburgh where passenger numbers were lower and didn't justify the use of a higher capacity wide-body aircraft. The 757 was also now able to operate from the US to Hawaii and on flights of around 4,000nm from Western Europe to the US east coast and Caribbean.

In July 1990 the RB.211-535R4 and RB.211-535C engines were approved for 180 minutes ETOPS. Several months earlier, the Pratt &Whitney PW2000 engines received 120 minutes ETOPS certification followed by 180 minutes ETOPS in April 1992.

Delta Air Lines, American Airlines and United Airlines eventually became the biggest operators of the 757. Delta Airlines ordered one hundred and sixteen 757-200s between 1980 and 1999. It also acquired forty-five 757-200s and sixteen 757-300s (its first and only 757-300s) following the merger with Northwest Airlines in 2008. Delta operated two hundred and five 757s after its first acquisition in 1984, the largest number of any airline. The 757 was also an important component of the American Airlines' fleet. The company ordered one hundred and twenty-six aircraft between 1988 and 1996 and went on to operate one hundred and seventy-seven 757-200s after acquiring 51 aircraft following mergers with TWA in 2001 and US Airways in 2015. United Airlines has operated one hundred and thirty-nine 757-200s and a small fleet of twenty-one 757-300s since 1989. All of its 757-300s and 41 757-200s were inherited from Continental Airlines when the two carriers merged in 2010. Other operators of the 757-200 in North America have included Allegiant Air (6), America West Airlines (15), American Trans Air (16 plus 12 757-300s), Canada 3000 Airlines (14), Nationair (10), North American Airlines (10), Ryan International Airlines (13 plus 2 757-300s), TWA (27) and US Airways (51).

Only a small number of orders for the 757 were gained from Asia, where airlines generally preferred larger wide-body aircraft. Singapore Airlines placed an order for four aircraft in May 1983. These were delivered the following year but, after only 5-6 years flying the 757, they were sold to American Trans Air. The expansion of airlines in China generated greater interest in the 757. An initial order for three aircraft in October 1987 from CAAC was followed by an order for three more the following year. These aircraft were eventually delivered to China Southern Airlines, the first one arriving in September 1987. China Southern Airlines became the largest operator of 757s on passenger services in China, using thirty-two aircraft until it retired the type in 2018. Shanghai Airlines was the next Chinese carrier to introduce the 757 into service, receiving its first example in August 1989 and going on to operate thirteen aircraft. Other operators of the 757 in China have included Air China (13), China Southwest Airlines (15) and Xiamen Air (9).

In Europe, the main customers for the 757-200 were British Airways, Iberia and Icelandair, all of which operated it on scheduled services. Iberia received its

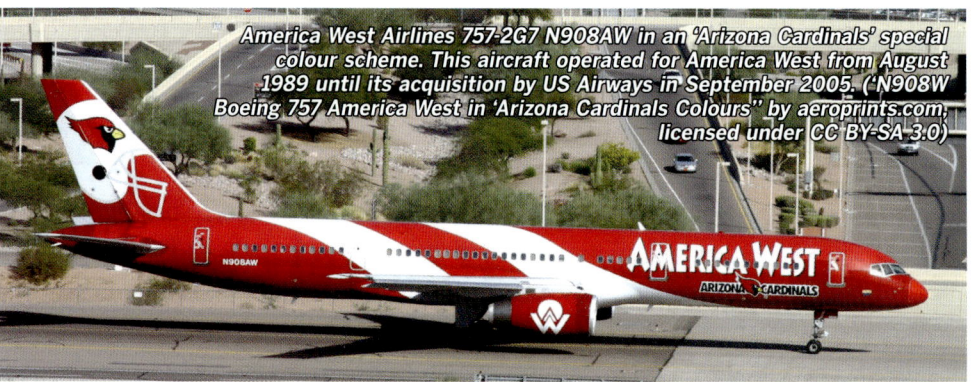

America West Airlines 757-2G7 N908AW in an 'Arizona Cardinals' special colour scheme. This aircraft operated for America West from August 1989 until its acquisition by US Airways in September 2005. ('N908W Boeing 757 America West in 'Arizona Cardinals Colours'' by aeroprints.com, licensed under CC BY-SA 3.0)

American Trans Air took delivery of 757-212 N751AT in May 1990 from Singapore Airlines. The carrier operated sixteen 757-200s. ('American Trans Air Boeing 757, N751AT BIK' by Aero Icarus, licensed under CC BY-SA 2.0)

Singapore Airlines 757-212 9V-SGN at Sultan Abdul Shah Airport, Kuala Lumpur, Malaysia. (LRS747)

China Southern Airlines Boeing 757-28S B-2830 on short final at Sheremetyevo Alexander S. Pushkin International Airport, Moscow. ('SouthernAirlines Boeing-757-200 SVO' by Sergey Kustov, licensed under CC BY-SA 3.0)

China Southwest Airlines acquired fifteen 757-200s between August 1992 and July 2002. 757-2Z0 B-2836, shown here, was in service with the carrier from February 1994 until January 2003. ('CHINA SOUTHWEST AIRLINES Boeing 757-2Z0' by contri, licensed under CC BY-SA 2.0)

Shanghai Airlines operated thirteen 757-200s, with its first aircraft received in August 1989. Shown here is the third example delivered to the carrier, B-2833. ('Shanghai Airlines Boeing 757-26D B-2833' by byeangel, licensed under CC BY-SA 2.0)

Xiamen Airlines Boeing 757-25C B-2848 at Shanghai Hongqiao Airport. This aircraft was in service with the airline from August 1995 to May 2015. ('B-2848 Boeing 757 Xiamen Airlines' by aeroprints.com, licensed under CC BY-SA 3.0)

Air China acquired Boeing 757-2Z0 B-2844 in March 2003. In 2014 it was converted to a freighter and continues to be operated by SF Airlines. ('Air China Boeing 757-2Z0 B-2844' by byeangel, licensed under CC BY-SA 2.0)

Icelandair 757-208 TF-FIH at Keflavik International Airport, Iceland, in May 1995. This aircraft was the first 757 to be delivered to the carrier in April 1990. (Kjell Oskar Granlund)

first 757 in November 1993, operating thirty aircraft before withdrawing the final ten 757s from service in 2006. The 757 became the main aircraft type in Icelandair's fleet during the 1990s following the acquisition of its first example in April 1990. The 757's unique attributes have been central to the successful development of Icelandair's extensive route network connecting Iceland to Europe and North America since the 1990s, and the carrier continues to operate the 757 today.

The 757-200 was very popular with European charter airlines operating inclusive tour services from northern Europe to the Mediterranean and further afield. As mentioned earlier, Monarch Airlines and Air Europe were the first carriers to use the 757-200 for charter services. Monarch Airlines operated a fleet of ten 757s between March 1983 and November 2014 and was the first airline to operate a 120 minute ETOPS flight by a 757 between Luton and Orlando via Gander, Newfoundland on 1 May 1988. Air Europe built up a fleet of seventeen 757-200s for its charter flights, which it also used on its scheduled route network before entering into administration in 1991.

German leisure airline, Condor, began operating the 757-200 in 1990 and used twenty of them over a period of sixteen years before switching to the 757-300 variant.

Other charter airlines that operated the 757-200 during the late-1980s and 1990s included Air 2000 (operated 27), Airtours International Airways (7), Air Holland (11), Britannia Airways (28), Caledonian Airways (8), Flying Colours (12), Inter European Airways (4) and LTU International Airways (12).

A period of rebranding and mergers of UK charter airlines and tour operators between 2000 and 2017 led to a large number of UK-based 757s changing owners and their appearance over the years. The merger

Iberia took delivery of thirty 757-200s between November 1993 and December 2008. The last to be received was 757-256 EC-HIX, seen here departing from Amsterdam's Schiphol Airport in March 2007. ('EC-HIX Iberia' by Pieter van Marion, licensed under CC BY-SA 2.0)

Boeing 757-230 D-ABND was delivered to Condor in May 1990. The carrier operated twenty 757-200s on its charter services until changing to the 757-300 variant from 2004. (LRS747)

Boeing 757-225 G-OOOV was operated by Air 2000 between February 1992 and September 2002. ('Air 2000 Boeing 757-225 G-OOOV by Kambui, licensed under CC BY-SA 2.0)

Airtours International Airways operated seven 757-200s including G-RJGR, seen here departing from Palma de Mallorca Airport in May 2000. (LRS747)

Boeing 757-204 G-BYAI was acquired by Britannia Airways in March 1993. It was subsequently transferred to Thomsonfly and then Thomson Airways until October 2010. ('Britannia Airways Boeing 757-204 G-BYAI' by Kambui, licensed under CC BY-SA 2.0)

Air Holland 757-27B, PH-AHE, at London Gatwick Airport. This aircraft was delivered to Air Holland in March 1988 and was operated by the carrier until March 2004, during which time it was leased out on at least six occasions. (Ewan Partridge)

Boeing 757-2Y0 G-CPEP was operated by First Choice Airways between March 2004 and May 2009. (Adrian Pingstone)

German carrier LTU International Airways operated twelve 757-200s including D-AMUI, seen here at Frankfurt International Airport in October 2000. ('LTU Boeing 757-2G5; D-AMUI@FRA' by Aero Icarus, licensed under CC BY-SA 2.0)

JMC Air was formed in 2000 following the merger of Caledonian Airways and Flying Colours. Shown here is 757-28A G-FCLD, a former Flying Colours aircraft, repainted in the JMC Air livery. (Don Gilham)

CHAPTER 3: COMMERCIAL PASSENGER SERVICE

Former airline Thomas Cook operated twenty-four 757s between March 2003 and April 2017, including 757-236 G-TCBB, shown here painted in 'Egypt, where it all begins' special colour scheme. (Author's collection)

Ex-First Choice Airways 757-28A G-OOBD was transferred to Thomson Airways in 2009 following the merger of First Choice and Thomsonfly. (Author's collection)

XL Airways took delivery of three 757-200s in November 2006, including G-VKND, shown here landing at Faro Airport, Portugal. ('Boeing 757-225, XL Airways' by Pedro Aragão, licensed under CC BY-SA 3.0)

English heavy metal band Iron Maiden leased 757-28A G-STRX from Astraeus Airlines in 2011 for use on its 'The Final Frontier World Tour 2011'. ('G-STRX Boeing 757 Astraeus in Iron Maiden C-s' by aeroprints.com, licensed under CC BY-SA 3.0)

of Flying Colours and Caledonian Airways in 2000 led to the formation of JMC Air, which subsequently rebranded to Thomas Cook Airlines in 2003. Airtours International was rebranded as MyTravel Airways in 2002 before becoming part of Thomas Cook Airlines in 2007. Britannia Airways was acquired by the TUI Group in 2000 and, as part of reorganisation of TUI operations in the UK, was rebranded Thomsonfly in 2004. First Choice Airways, which had been created from the rebranding of Air 2000 in 2004, merged with Thomsonfly to form Thomson Airways in 2008. Thomson Airways was renamed TUI Airways in 2017.

Thomas Cook used nineteen 757-200s between March 2003 and January 2016. It also operated five 757-300s, retiring the last one in January 2019. TUI Airways operated fourteen 757-200s from 2017. It withdrew one aircraft from service in October 2018 followed by four in 2019 and six during 2020. The remaining three operated the 2021 summer season before being retired in September and October of that year.

Other UK carriers which have operated the 757 since the turn of the century include Astraeus Airways, Jet2, Titan Airways and XL Airways.

Boeing 757-300

The 757-300 was initially ordered by Condor in 1996, followed by orders from Icelandair and Arkia Israeli Airlines. The 757-300 entered service with Condor on 19 March 1999. The carrier went on to acquire thirteen examples to mainly serve its short- and medium-haul routes to popular holiday destinations in Europe and North Africa. Arkia received its two 757-300s in January/February 2000 and a single aircraft went to Icelandair in March 2002.

American Trans Air/ATA placed an order for twelve 757-300s in June 2000, and after several years of reliable service with Condor, the 757-300 began to establish a foothold in the US market. Orders were placed for sixteen aircraft from Northwest Airlines and fifteen (later reduced to nine) from Continental Airlines in 2001. British charter carrier, JMC Airlines, also placed an order for two aircraft in April 2001. Boeing also strongly promoted the 757-300 to two of its largest customers, American Airlines and United Airlines, as a potential replacement for their Boeing 767-200s, but neither had sufficient financial resources to order it.

American Trans Air/ATA was the North American launch customer for the 757-300, receiving its first two aircraft in August 2001. Due to financial problems, and in an attempt to reduce operating costs, ATA's eventual fleet of twelve aircraft were returned to Boeing between June 2005 and April 2008 for refurbishment before being leased to Continental Airlines. In 2010 they were absorbed by United Airlines after its merger with Continental, together with the nine 757-300s that had been delivered directly from Boeing between December 2001 and April 2004.

Condor received its first 757-300 D-ABOE, shown here, on 10 March 1999. The aircraft was withdrawn from use by Condor in November 2022 and is currently with Skyline Express Airlines. (John Visanich)

Israeli charter airline Arkia operated two 757-300s. The first one (4X-BAU) was delivered in January 2000 and is shown here at Geneva Airport in 2007. ('Arkia Boeing 757-300; 4X-BAU@GVA;24.02.2007' by Aero Icarus, from Zürich, licensed under CC BY-SA 2.0)

One of two 757-300s operated by Icelandair, TF-FIX was delivered as new in March 2002 and remains active in 2023. ('Icelandair Boeing 757-308 TF-FIX 'Hengill' by Kambui, licensed under CC BY-SA 2.0)

American Trans Air was the North American launch customer for the 757-300. The carrier received its first example, N550TZ shown here, in August 2001. (John Olafson)

Boeing 757-324 N75853 was delivered to Continental Airlines in February 2002. It now operates for United Airlines after the United-Continental merger in 2010. ('N75853' by Eddie Maloney, licensed under CC BY-SA 2.0)

Delta Air Lines 757-351 N588NW departing from Los Angeles International Airport. This aircraft was originally delivered to Northwest Airlines in February 2003 before being transferred to Delta Air Lines in October 2008 following the completion of a merger. ('N588NW LAX' by Eric Salard, licensed under CC BY-SA 2.0)

Northwest Airlines took delivery of its first 757-300 in July 2002 and acquired a further fifteen by October 2003, all of which were transferred to Delta Airlines in October 2008 following the completion of a merger.

By the early 2000s Boeing was faced with declining sales of the 757 and, despite the launch of the 757-300, the continued viability of the 757 programme was in doubt. A switch to smaller aircraft, such as the Airbus A320 and Boeing 737, due to the downturn in the airline industry following the 9/11 terrorist attacks in the US, was a major factor behind the diminishing sales. A sales campaign in 2003, focusing on the 757-300 and 757-200PF, only resulted in five new orders. Subsequent to Continental Airlines' decision in October 2003 to switch the remainder of its 757-300 order (six aircraft) to the 737-800, Boeing announced the end of 757 production. The manufacturer built 1050 757s between 1981 and 2004, of which 913 were 757-200s (plus one prototype), 81 freighters and 55 757-300s. The last 757 to be built, a 757-200 for Shanghai Airlines, rolled off the production line at Renton on 28 October 2004 and was delivered on 28 November 2005, after several months of storage.

The use of the 757 as a passenger aircraft has slowly declined in subsequent years as operators have begun to replace it with smaller, more efficient types, such as the Airbus A320 and A321 and the Boeing 737-800 and -900. The sharp rise in fuel prices between 2004 and 2008 had a significant impact on short- to medium-haul services, especially in the US. American Airlines, at one time the second largest operator of the 757, began to retire some of its older 757s in 2012, although it still planned to continue to operate the type until 2024. However, in March 2020, the outbreak of the coronavirus pandemic led to American Airlines accelerating the retirement plan. It announced that all 757s were to be phased out by the end of 2021. In the end, its remaining 34 aircraft were put into storage between January and the end of March 2020 and never operated for American again.

Both Delta Air Lines and United Airlines have withdrawn a number of their 757-200s from service annually since 2008 (Delta) and 2011 (United Airlines). In 2023, just over 70% of United Airlines' 757-200s have been removed from the fleet, whereas over 50% of Delta's 757-200s still remain in service. It is expected that both carriers will continue to operate the 757 through to the mid-late 2020s.

In Europe, the first 757 was withdrawn from Iberia in 1997 after four years' service. Some of the remaining twenty-nine aircraft were withdrawn each year from 2000 until the end of 757 operations in 2006. British Airways retired its last 757 in 2010.

Despite the diminishing number of 757 passenger aircraft in service, numerous aircraft have been converted to continue to fly as freighters, especially since the boom in air cargo operations from 2020 onwards (see Chapter 6).

The 757 in 2023

About a quarter of the 968 passenger-carrying 757s that were built remain in service today. Almost 75% of the active 757s are operated by Delta Air Lines and United Airlines. Delta is the largest remaining operator with one hundred and six active 757-200s and sixteen 757-300s, while United Airlines still operates around forty 757-200s and twenty-one 757-300s. In December 2019, United Airlines ordered fifty Airbus A321XLRs with delivery expected from 2024. The A321XLR is seen as an ideal replacement for the 757.

Boeing 757-330 G-JMOF operating for Thomas Cook Airlines during the summer season 2017, on lease from Condor. (Author's collection)

Roll-out of the last 757 to be built on 28 October 2004, a 757-200 for Shanghai Airlines. (Boeing)

The final 757 to be built, 757-26D B-2876, seen here operating for Shanghai Airlines. B-2876 was delivered on 28 November 2005. ('Shanghai Airlines Boeing 757-26D B-2876' by byeangel, licensed under CC BY-SA 2.0)

Delta Air Lines is the largest remaining operator of the 757. Shown here is 757-251 N539US landing at Hartsfield–Jackson International Airport, Atlanta in 2023. (Matt Falcus)

United Airlines 757-224 N14102 painted in 'Her Art Here: Corinne Antonelli (New York/New Jersey)' special colour scheme. (Mike Kell)

In 2022 Condor introduced a new striped colour scheme for its fleet. Boeing 757-330 D-ABOI is shown painted in the 'Condor Sea' theme. (Paul Miot-Paschke/Condor)

In Europe, Icelandair, Condor and Jet2 remain major operators of the 757. Icelandair has thirteen of its fleet of fourteen passenger 757-200s and both 757-300s currently in active service. It plans to replace its 757 fleet with fuel-efficient Airbus A321LRs and A321XLRs from 2025. For Condor, eight of its nine 757-300s remain in active service. However, the carrier ordered thirteen Airbus A320neos and twenty-eight A321neos in 2022, with delivery scheduled from 2024, which will lead to the withdrawal of its 757s. Jet2 is currently operating eight 757-200s (see Chapter 5).

Another significant user of the 757-200 is Azur Air of the Russian Federation. The carrier has a fleet of ten aircraft, of which eight are reportedly in service. Azerbaijan Airlines and Privilege Style of Spain each have one 757-200 in service.

Several operators currently have small numbers of 757-200s recorded as parked and not in active service, including Skyline Express Airlines, New Pacific Airlines, Sunday Airlines of Kazakhstan and Turkmenistan Airlines. These aircraft may never re-enter service.

In 2023, Icelandair continues to be a major operator of the 757 in Europe. Its fleet of 757-200s includes TF-FIU painted in the eye-catching 'Aurora (Northern Lights)' special colour scheme. (Author's collection)

Azur Air of the Russian Federation currently has a fleet of ten 757-200s. 757-2Q8 RA-73071 was acquired in December 2014 and originally registered as VQ-BEZ. It was re-registered in April 2022. ('RA-73071 Boeing 757-200 Azur VKO 2022-08-03' by Mike1979 Russia, licensed under CC BY-SA 4.0)

United Airlines 757-33N N57870 at Los Angeles International Airport. United Airlines continue to operate up to twenty 757-300s in 2023. ('United Airlines Boeing 757-33N(WL), N57870 – LAX' by Eric Salard, licensed under CC BY-SA 2.0)

Chapter 4:

British Airways and the Boeing 757

British Airways, along with Eastern Air Lines, placed the first orders for the Boeing 757-200. They both opted for the Rolls-Royce RB211-535 engine. British Airways' initial order for nineteen aircraft was signed in March 1979. Its decision to buy the Boeing 757 was somewhat controversial. British Airways was looking for a replacement for its uneconomical Hawker Siddeley Trident 3B aircraft, which had been the mainstay of its short-haul fleet. The Trident also had to be replaced by 1986 due to noise regulations. There were two potential contenders: the Boeing 757 and the Airbus A310, both newly developed airliners. There was a strong feeling in the UK government at the time that British Airways should buy the A310 to support the European aviation industry. However, Boeing offered the opportunity for Rolls-Royce to be a partner on the 7N7 (757) project by providing the RB211-535 as the favoured lead engine for the aircraft. It is believed that this involvement in the project by a British company clinched the initial order from British Airways for the 757 as the A310 was only available with American manufactured engines.

British Airways also faced some difficulties with the pilots' unions, which argued that the 757 was operated by a flight crew of three, similar to the Trident that it was replacing. After negotiations, a resolution and acceptance of a two-pilot crew was agreed in 1981.

An early change in British Airways' original order of nineteen aircraft occurred in June 1982, before the first aircraft had been delivered, when two aircraft slots were sold to charter airline Air Europe. At the time this was very beneficial to British Airways as they were

British Airways 757-236 G-BIKB following the first revenue flight to Edinburgh in 1983. ('G-BIKB Boeing 757-236 British Airways' by aceebee, licensed under CC BY-SA 2.0)

CHAPTER 4: BRITISH AIRWAYS AND THE BOEING 757

facing heavy financial losses due to the economic recession of the early 1980s and were under pressure to cut the 757 order to reduce capital expenditure. The deal saved the airline nearly £40m over two years and included British Airways providing Air Europe with flight crews, access to simulator facilities, spares and technical support.

British Airways' first Boeing 757-236 was delivered on 25 January 1983. It was registered as G-BIKB and named 'Windsor Castle'. Most of the 757 fleet were named after historic British castles until British Airways stopped the practice of naming aircraft in the late 1990s. The second aircraft, G-BIKC, 'Edinburgh Castle', arrived three days later and the two aircraft were used for crew training and route-proving flights for a week, in preparation for going into service. The first commercial flight of a British Airways B757 took place on 9 February 1983 and was operated by G-BIKB on the Shuttle service from London Heathrow to Belfast.

Five aircraft had been delivered to British Airways by April 1983, although one (G-BIKF) was leased to Air Europe for the summer months. The configuration of the aircraft was a six-abreast, two-class layout, comprising Club and Tourist, with a total of one hundred and eighty-nine seats. The 757s were fully active, operating the Shuttle routes between London Heathrow and Belfast, Glasgow, Edinburgh and Manchester. European services from Heathrow to Rome, Paris, Milan and Copenhagen were flown by the 757 for the first time in the late spring and summer of 1983, expanding to Athens, Amsterdam, Nice and Frankfurt in October, and Geneva and Zurich in January 1984. By early 1984, the fleet of 757s had increased to ten and the airline confirmed the option to acquire three more aircraft in 1985. The 757 was

The second 757-236 to be delivered to British Airways at the end of January 1983 was G-BIKC and it was named 'Edinburgh Castle'. ('G-BIKC Boeing 757-236 British Airways' by Colin Cooke, licensed under CC BY-SA 2.0)

British Airways 757-236 G-BIKH with the Golden Khokhloma colour scheme painted on the tail fin. ('British Airways Boeing 757-236; G-BIKH@ZRH;23.06.1998' by Aero Icarus, licensed under CC BY-SA 2.0)

British Airways 757-236 G-BIKO taxiing at Zurich Airport in February 1998. ('British Airways Boeing 757-236, G-BIKO@ZRH' by Aero Icarus, licensed under CC BY-SA 2.0)

Boeing 757-236 G-BMRA was delivered to British Airways in March 1987 and remained in service with the carrier until December 2001. ('British Airways Boeing 757-236; G-BMRA@ZRH;16.05.2000' by Aero Icarus, licensed under CC BY-SA 2.0)

G-BMRC at Zurich Airport in July 1995, resplendent in British Airways' Landor livery. ('British Airways Boeing 757-236; G-BMRC@ZRH;12.07.1995' by Aero Icarus, licensed under CC BY-SA 2.0)

Boeing 757-236 G-BMRF painted in the 'Water Dreaming' scheme. ('British Airways Boeing 757-236 G-BMRF 'Water Dreaming' by Kambui, licensed under CC BY-SA 2.0)

proving a success, with a lower fuel burn (by at least 30%) than the Trident Two and Trident Three it had replaced and noise levels reduced by more than 40%.

British Airways continued to slowly and progressively develop the 757 fleet, with orders for two more aircraft in April 1987, three in August 1987 and one in the latter part of 1988. For the first time the up-rated RB 211-535E4 engines were employed, which were considered to contribute up to an 11% saving in fuel consumption over the previously supplied RB 211-535C powerplants. A further five RB211-535E4 powered 757s were ordered in October 1990. As new aircraft were delivered, some were reconfigured with an additional twelve seats (total of 201 seats) and used specifically for domestic Shuttle operations. Most aircraft remained in the two-class European layout, although a number of changes were introduced in 1994, including a new Club Europe Business Class. The forward cabin and part of the mid-cabin area was changed to a five-abreast layout, with wider, leather seats and extra legroom. This reduced the maximum seating to 180, but it was relatively easy to change this configuration back to six-abreast economy seating if required.

During 1984 and 1985 British Airways used some of its 757s to operate charter and scheduled leisure flights for various tour operators from Manchester, Belfast and Glasgow. Destinations included Tenerife, Venice, Ibiza, Rhodes, Las Palmas, Athens and Malta. Overnight scheduled services were also operated from Manchester to Athens, Larnaca and Malta. Another operation carried out by British Airways' 757s until late 1992 was the night-time Royal Mail service between Heathrow and Edinburgh. An aircraft departed from each airport before midnight. On arrival the mail was unloaded and the aircraft was in position to resume Shuttle duties early the following morning

CHAPTER 4: BRITISH AIRWAYS AND THE BOEING 757

In 1986, the RB211-535E4-powered 757 was approved for Extended-range Twin-engine Operational Performance Standards (ETOPS), which was particularly relevant for Caledonian Airways, British Airways's charter subsidiary. Between 1989 and 1995, Caledonian operated six of BA's newly acquired 757s and named them after Scottish Lochs. The first aircraft delivered to Caledonian (G-BPEA) was the first British Airways 757 to have maximum take-off weights and the up-rated RB211-535E4 engines. This allowed Caledonian to operate a number of charter flights to the USA, Canada and Thailand from Gatwick Airport, although most of Caledonian's operations took place within Europe, with the aircraft configured in a high-density, 233-seat arrangement.

British Airways also used 757s on some transatlantic routes in the mid-1990s. Three aircraft were fitted with new Club World seats in the forward cabin and a more spacious World Traveller economy layout in the rest of the cabin, giving a seating arrangement for a total of one hundred and fifty-six passengers. These aircraft were used on daily services: from Glasgow to New York JFK and onwards to Boston, from Birmingham to New York JFK and on to Toronto, and from Manchester to New York JFK. However, these long haul routes proved not to be financially viable and the operations ended in November 1998 with the aircraft returning to short-haul operations.

Despite various attempts at route diversification, for the majority of the time British Airways operated the 757 on European routes from Heathrow to a range of locations and as far afield as Larnaca, Lisbon, Helsinki and Tel Aviv. Several aircraft were based at Gatwick Airport during the late 1990s, but this became only a short-term arrangement after British Airways reorganised its route network and standardised Boeing 737 operations at Gatwick and Boeing 757 operations from Heathrow.

Displaying the 'Rendevous' scheme, G-BMRG was acquired by British Airways in May 1988. ('British Airways Boeing 757-236 G-BMRG 'Rendezvous' by Kambui, licensed under CC BY-SA 2.0)

British Airways 757-236 G-BPEA was the first aircraft of six 757-200s to be operated by Caledonian Airways, British Airways' charter subsidiary, between 1989 and 1995. Caledonian named the 757s after Scottish Lochs, with G-BPEA called 'Loch of the Clans'. G-BPEA was the first British Airways 757-236 to have maximum take-off weights and the up-rated RB211-535E4 engines. (LRS747)

Boeing 757-236 G-BPEE 'Loch Tay' operating for Caledonian Airways in July 1994. ('Boeing 757-236, Caledonian Airways' by Pedro Aragão licensed under CC BY-SA 3.0)

The number of aircraft in British Airways' 757 fleet peaked at fifty-three in 1999, but the airline had already taken a decision which marked the beginning of the end of the 757 in British Airways' service. Towards the end of 1998, British Airways decided to use smaller-capacity aircraft from the Airbus A320 family on its short-haul routes for profitability reasons. It introduced seven A320s into service during 1988 and 1989 and four A319s in 1999, and ordered the larger A321 which was seen as a direct replacement for some of the 757s. Four 757 aircraft that were still on order and due to be delivered in 1999 were cancelled and sold to National Airlines. In October 1999, British Airways announced that thirty-four of its 757 fleet had been sold to Boeing Airplane Services for special freighter conversion before being leased to DHL International or their subsidiary, European Air Transport Leipzig (EAT). The first aircraft to leave the fleet on the 19 May 2000 was G-BIKA ('Dover Castle'); it was the third aircraft originally delivered to British Airways in 1983. As British Airways worked to reduce its overall aircraft fleet, especially after the 9/11 terrorist attacks, many 757s were placed in storage until they could be transferred to their new owners for freighter conversion. By December 2001, twenty-five aircraft had been withdrawn.

By 2004, only thirteen 757s remained. The opening of Terminal 5 at London Heathrow in March 2008 led to the disappearance of more or less all the 757s from British Airways' domestic Shuttle routes. Terminal 5's baggage system was set up to use only baggage containers in order to speed up loading and unloading. Bulk-loading of baggage and cargo only ever took place on the 757, so these aircraft were transferred to Terminal 3 where they were largely used on services to Madrid, Barcelona, Lisbon, Nice, Helsinki, Vienna and Malaga.

The final month of operations by the British Airways 757s was in October 2010, when only three aircraft remained. The final flights were on 30 October 2010 and included G-CPET, the last Boeing 757 aircraft to be retired from the main British Airways fleet, which was repainted in the original 757 Negus livery and named 'Stokesay Castle' to mark the type's retirement. It operated farewell Shuttle flights between Heathrow and Manchester, Glasgow and lastly Edinburgh.

The Boeing 757 was operated by British Airways for twenty-seven years between 1983 and 2010, during which time it flew over 1.9 million hours. Despite some political and economic concerns when it was first ordered by British Airways, it was one of the most favoured aircraft of British Airways' short-haul fleet throughout its time in service.

British Airways Boeing 757 Fleet (Source: Planespotters.net)

Registration	C/n	Name	Delivery Date	Exit date	Fate
G-BIKA	22172	Dover Castle	28/03/1983	19/05/2000	to EAT
G-BIKB	22173	Windsor Castle	25/01/1983	25/08/2001	to EAT
G-BIKC	22174	Edinburgh Castle	31/01/1983	17/04/2001	to DHL
G-BIKD	22175	Caernarfon Castle	10/03/1983	03/05/2001	to EAT
G-BIKF	22177	Carrickfergus Castle	28/04/1983	03/06/2002	to DHL
G-BIKG	22178	Stirling Castle	26/08/1983	07/07/2001	to DHL
G-BIKH	22179	Richmond Castle	18/10/1983	22/03/2001	to EAT
G-BIKI	22180	Tintagel Castle	30/11/1983	15/09/2000	to EAT
G-BIKJ	22181	Conwy Castle	09/01/1984	01/07/2000	to EAT
G-BIKK	22182	Eilean Donan Castle	01/02/1984	11/06/2001	to DHL
G-BIKL	22183	Nottingham Castle	29/02/1984	07/08/2001	to EAT
G-BIKM	22184	Glamis Castle	21/03/1984	06/01/2002	to DHL
G-BIKN	22186	Bodiam Castle	23/01/1985	20/11/2001	to DHL
G-BIKO	22187	Harlech Castle	14/02/1985	01/02/2002	to DHL
G-BIKP	22188	Enniskillen Castle	11/03/1985	14/02/2001	to DHL
G-BIKR	22189	Bamburgh Castle	29/03/1985	20/07/2002	to EAT
G-BIKS	22190	Corfe Castle	31/05/1985	31/03/2002	to DHL
G-BIKT	23398	Carisbrooke Castle	01/11/1985	09/01/2003	to EAT
G-BIKU	23399	Inveraray Castle	07/11/1985	27/10/2001	to DHL
G-BIKV	23400	Raglan Castle	09/12/1985	14/11/2001	to DHL
G-BIKW	23492	Belvoir Castle	07/03/1986	30/09/2001	to EAT
G-BIKX	23493	Warwick Castle	14/03/1986	27/06/2001	to EAT
G-BIKY	23533	Leeds Castle	28/03/1986	31/12/2002	to EAT
G-BIKZ	23532	Kenilworth Castle	15/05/1986	11/09/2001	to DHL
G-BKRM	22176	'Braemar Castle'	LSD from Air Europe: 01/11/1984-30/04/1986 and 02/11/1986-26/04/1987		
G-BMRA	23710	Beaumaris Castle	02/03/1987	14/12/2001	to DHL
G-BMRB	23975	Colchester Castle	25/09/1987	31/07/2002	to DHL
G-BMRC	24072	Rochester Castle	22/01/1988	29/03/2002	to DHL
G-BMRD	24073	Bothwell Castle	29/02/1988	16/01/2002	to DHL

Boeing 757 · Timelines

Registration	C/n	Name	Delivery Date	Exit date	Fate
G-BMRE	24074	Killyleagh Castle	23/03/1988	24/02/2002	to DHL
G-BMRF	24101	Hever Castle	13/05/1988	04/10/2001	to DHL
G-BMRG	24102	Caerphilly Castle	31/05/1988	31/12/2001	to EAT
G-BMRH	24266	Norwich Castle	21/02/1989	31/03/2002	to DHL
G-BMRI	24267	Tonbridge Castle	17/02/1989	30/03/2002	to EAT
G-BMRJ*	24268	Old Wardour Castle (Caledonian: Loch Tummel)	06/03/1989	10/03/2002	to DHL
G-BPEA*	24370	Kidwelly Castle (Caledonian: Loch of the Clans)	31/03/1989	04/04/2001	to Pegasus Aviation
G-BPEB*	24371	(Caledonian: Loch Lomond)	27/04/1989	28/02/2001	to Pegasus Aviation
G-BPEC*	24882	Sir Simon Rattle (Caledonian: Loch Katrine)	06/11/1990	06/05/2009	to FedEx
G-BPED	25059	Blair Castle	30/04/1991	13/09/2009	to FedEx
G-BPEE*	25060	Robert Louis Stevenson (Caledonian: Loch Tay)	03/05/1991	19/11/2009	to FedEx
G-BPEF*	24120	(Caledonian: Loch Fainnach)	18/05/1992	15/04/2003	to Sun d'Or
G-BPEI	25806	Winchester Castle	09/03/1994	30/10/2009	to FedEx
G-BPEJ	25807	Llangollen Castle	25/04/1994	06/08/2008	to OpenSkies
G-BPEK	25808	Cardew Castle	17/03/1995	15/02/2008	to OpenSkies
G-CPEL	24398	Walmer Castle	24/08/1992	19/05/2009	to FedEx
G-CPEM	28665	Un-named	28/03/1997	01/05/2010	to FedEx
G-CPEN	28666	Un-named	23/04/1997	20/12/2009	to FedEx
G-CPEO	28667	Un-named	11/07/1997	30/06/2010	to FedEx
G-CPEP	25268	Un-named	17/04/1997	30/04/2002	to Air 2000
G-CPER	29113	Un-named	29/12/1997	30/10/2010	to FedEx
G-CPES	29114	Un-named	17/03/1998	30/10/2010	to FedEx
G-CPET	29115	'Stokesay Castle'	12/05/1998	06/11/2010	to FedEx
G-CPEU#	29941	Un-named	01/05/1999	31/10/2002	to Air 2000
G-CPEV#	29943	Un-named	11/06/1999	20/12/2002	to Air 2000
G-DRJC	23895	'Braemar Castle'	Lsd from Monarch Airlines 26/04/1988-19/04/1989		
G-OOOB	23822	Un-named	Lsd from Air 2000 01/11/1987-23/04/1988		

* aircraft operated by Caledonian Airways during part of BA service
\# aircraft leased rather than purchased by BA

CHAPTER 4: BRITISH AIRWAYS AND THE BOEING 757

British Airways 757-236 G-BPEI painted in the Chatham Dockyard livery. (Adrian Pingstone)

The colourful 'Animals and Trees' South Africa scheme painted on the tail fin of 757-236 G-CPEL, shown at Zurich Airport in September 2002. ('G-CPEL B757-236 British Aws (Animals&Trees) ZRH 04SEP02' by Ken Fielding, licensed under CC BY-SA 3.0)

British Airways 757-236 G-CPES taxiing at Amsterdam Schiphol Airport in December 2003. ('G-CPES British Airways' by Pieter van Marion, licensed under CC BY-SA 2.0)

Boeing 757-236 G-CPEO was operated by British Airways from July 1997 to June 2010 before being converted to a freighter for use by FedEx. ('British Airways Boeing 757-236 G-CPEO 'Whale Rider' by Kambui, licensed under CC BY-SA 2.0)

The first 757 to leave British Airways' fleet was G-BIKA, in May 2000. It is shown here at Zurich Airport in 1998. ('British Airways Boeing 757-236; G-BIKA@ZRH;04.07.1998' by Aero Icarus, licensed under CC BY-SA 2.0)

The final 757 in service with British Airways was G-CPET which was withdrawn in November 2010. ('Boeing 757-236, British Airways' by Pedro Aragão, licensed under CC BY-SA 3.0)

Chapter 5:

Britain's last operator of passenger 757s: Jet2.com and the Boeing 757

Jet2.com is the last British airline to operate passenger-carrying 757s. The low-cost leisure airline was originally established in January 1978 as Express Air Services, a small cargo carrier which operated freight services between Bournemouth Airport and the Channel Islands. Following the award of Royal Mail contracts in the early 1980s and the purchase of the company by the Dart Group in 1983, the carrier was renamed Channel Express. Charter passenger services were subsequently introduced and, in 2002, Channel Express established its low-cost brand, Jet2, renamed Jet2.com in 2006. Jet2.com has expanded to become a major carrier, operating scheduled and charter flights to an extensive range of destinations from eleven bases in the UK.

Jet2 acquired its first two 757-200s in May 2005 and introduced the type into service in October 2005, operating between Leeds-Bradford and Tenerife South Airport. The 757 fleet increased to nine aircraft by the end of 2006, after the purchase of six aircraft and one taken on lease from GATX for three months. Single additions followed in 2008 and 2010 from Thomsonfly and ATA Airlines respectively. At this point, Jet2.com was the owner of all its 757s. However, in early 2011 they leased two aircraft (G-LSAL and G-LSAM) from Allegiant Air, increasing the fleet size to thirteen. At the end of the 2012 summer season, G-LSAL and G-LSAM were returned to the lessor and the fleet was reduced to eleven aircraft. In order to add additional capacity for the 2015 summer season, Jet2.com wet-leased a 757-200 from Spanish charter airline Privilege Style. A similar arrangement in 2016 and 2018, resulted in the wet-leasing of a 757-200 from Titan Airways.

The first retirement of an aircraft from the 757 fleet occurred in November 2019. Following the suspension of air travel due to the outbreak of the COVID-19 pandemic in early 2020, Jet2.com retired two more 757s in March 2020 and the rest of the fleet were put into storage. The resumption of some passenger flights in mid-July 2020 led to the return to service of four 757s until the end of October when there was another period of long-term storage until the

Jet2.com 757-236 G-LSAA was one of the first two 757s to be acquired by Jet2's parent company, Channel Express, in May 2005. (Author's collection)

Boeing 757-27B G-LSAB being towed to a gate at Manchester Airport in preparation for departure. (Jet2.com)

Jet2.com 757-23A G-LSAC was acquired in March 2006 and entered into service with Jet2 several months later. (Author's collection)

beginning of July 2021. Jet2.com gradually returned some 757s back into service, initially operating two in July 2021 and building up to five by the end of the year. It wasn't until June 2022 that all eight 757s in the fleet were fully operational again. Several of the older 757s were parked for at least three months of the quieter 2022/23 winter season, with a full complement of eight aircraft back in service by March 2023. The active aircraft were G-LSAA, G-LSAB, G-LSAC, G-LSAE, G-LSAI, G-LSAJ, G-LSAK and G-LSAN. G-LSAA was permanently withdrawn from use on the 10 November 2023.

The age of Jet2.com's current 757 fleet ranges from 27.2 to 36.2 years (as of January 2024). All of the 757s are powered by Rolls-Royce RB.211-535E4 engines. They are operated in a single economy-class seating configuration accommodating up to 235 passengers. During the summer season Jet2.com normally operates the 757s on short-haul flights to its more popular, high-demand destinations, such as Alicante, Malaga, Ibiza, Faro and Mallorca, as well as on longer routes to destinations, including Tenerife, Lanzarote, Gran Canaria, Fuerteventura, Crete, Cyprus, Paphos, Kos, Rhodes, Corfu, Zakynthos, Bodrum and Antalya. In the winter season, the 757s usually operate to winter sun destinations, in particular Tenerife, Lanzarote, Gran Canaria and Fuerteventura, and less frequently to Alicante, Malaga and Faro, as well as flying skiers to Geneva.

Although Jet2.com has not announced any specific plans for the retirement of its elderly 757 fleet, in August 2021 the carrier confirmed an order for thirty-six Airbus A321neos and increased the order to fifty-seven aircraft (plus eighteen options) by April the following year, stating that one of the reasons for the order was 'to refresh its existing aircraft fleet'.

Delivery of the first A321neo took place in May 2023. Additional deliveries are likely to span five years until 2028. Furthermore, an order for thirty-five A320neos, including an option for an additional thirty-six aircraft, was announced in October 2022, therefore, it would appear that the Jet2.com's 757's days are numbered.

Departing from runway 23R at Manchester Airport is Jet2.com's 757-236 G-LSAD. (Author's collection)

Jet2.com 757-27B G-LSAE painted in a white and blue scheme known as Jet2 Holidays colours. (Author's collection)

Former China Southern Airlines 757-21B was acquired by Jet2.com in November 2006 and registered as G-LSAG. It was operated by the carrier for thirteen years before eventually being broken up at Cotswold Airport in January 2021. (Author's collection)

G-LSAA (c/n 24122) 757-236 First Flight: 19 Jul 1988	Delivered to Air Europe in July 1988. Operated by Air Europa from November 1988 and returned to Air Europe in May1989. Used by Air Europa from May 1991 then to Iberia in April 1998. To Air Anatolia in April 2002 and Fly Air from April 2003 before returning to lessor in March 2004. Acquired by Channel Express in May 2005 and transferred to Jet2. Withdrawn from use in November 2023.
G-LSAB (c/n 24136) 757-27B First Flight: 11 Mar 1988	Delivered to Air Holland in March 1988 (with leases to Odyssey International and Sterling Airways). Sold to Britannia Airways in May 1991. To El Al Israel Airlines in May 1996 and Martinair from April 2000. Returned to Air Holland in May 2001 followed by Air Anatolia from April 2002 and to Fly Air in May 2003. Acquired by Channel Express in May 2005 and transferred to Jet2.
G-LSAC (c/n 25488) 757-23A First Flight: 10 Jul 1992	Delivered to Air Transat on lease in November 1992. Leased by Ryan International Airlines from January 2003. Acquired by the Dart Group in March 2006 and operated by Jet2 from May 2006.
G-LSAD (c/n 24397) 757-236 First Flight: 30 Mar 1989	Delivered to Air Europe in April 1989. Operated by Air Europa from October 1989 and returned to Air Europe in October1990. To Air 2000 in May 1991 and Greece Airways from April 2004 (with lease to Air Scotland). Acquired by Jet2 in June 2006. Withdrawn from use in March 2020 and broken up at Cotswold Airport in August 2022.
G-LSAE (c/n 24135) 757-27B First Flight: 19 Feb 1988	Delivered to Air Holland in March 1988 (with leases to Sterling Airways, Icelandair, Dinar Lineas Aereas, Spanair and Air Gabon). To Air Slovakia in July 2004. Acquired by Jet2 in September 2006.
G-LSAF (c/n 22689) 757-225 First Flight: 4 Dec 1986	Delivered to Eastern Air Lines in December 1986. To LTE International Airways in February 1990. Used on lease by LTU from October 1993, Atlas International from May 2001and Atlasjet from May 2003. Acquired by Jet2 on lease from GATX in October 2006. Returned to lessor in January 2007.
G-LSAG (c/n 24014) 757-21B First Flight: 31 Aug 1987	Delivered to CAAC Airlines in September 1987. Used from November 1990 by China Southern Airlines. Acquired by Jet2 in November 2006. Withdrawn from use in November 2019 and broken up at Cotswold Airport in January 2021.
G-LSAH (c/n 24015) 757-21B First Flight: 8 Oct 1987	Delivered to CAAC Airlines in October 1987. Used from November 1990 by China Southern Airlines. Acquired by Jet2 in November 2006. Withdrawn from use in March 2020 and stored at Cotswold Airport pending scrapping.
G-LSAI (c/n 24016) 757-21B First Flight: 8 Oct 1987	Delivered to China Southern Airlines in November 1987. Acquired by Jet2 in November 2006.

G-LSAJ (c/n 24793) 757-236 First Flight: 7 June 1990	Delivered to Air Europe in June 1990 (with lease to Air Europa). To Air 2000 in May 1991. Used on lease from ACG by Blue Scandinavia from December 1997, Britannia Airways Sweden from January 1998, Britannia Airways UK from April 2002, Thomsonfly from November 2004, Britannia Airways Sweden from March 2005, TUIfly Nordic from May 2006 and Thomsonfly from March 2008. Acquired by Jet2 in May 2008.
G-LSAK (c/n 27973) 757-23N First Flight: 6 Nov 1996	Delivered to American Trans Air/ATA Airlines in November 1996. Acquired by Jet2 in January 2010. Wet-leased to RAK Airways from September 2011 to June 2012.
G-LSAL (c/n 26967) 757-204 First Flight: 26 Jan 1993	Delivered to Britannia Airways in March 1993. Used on lease from AerCap by Thomsonfly from November 2004 and Thomson Airways from May 2009. Acquired by Jet2 on lease from Allegiant Air in February 2011. Returned to lessor in October 2012.
G-LSAM (c/n 26966) 757-204 First Flight: 21 Jan 1993	Delivered to Britannia Airways in February 1993. Used on lease by Thomsonfly from November 2004 and Thomson Airways from May 2009. Acquired by Jet2 on lease from Allegiant Air in March 2011. Returned to lessor in November 2012.
G-LSAN (c/n 26635) 757-2K2(WL) First Flight: 30 Mar 1994	Delivered to Transavia in April 1994. Used on lease from GECAS by ATA Airlines from November 2003 and Axis Airways from April 2005. To OceanAir in December 2007, Avianca from October 2008 and AeroGal from March 2010. Acquired by Jet2 in May 2012.
G-POWH (c/n 29308) 757-256 First Flight: 5 Jul 2000	Wet-leased from Titan Airways, March-October 2016 and May-September 2018.
EC-ISY (c/n 26241) 757-256 First Flight: 5 Aug 1993	Wet-leased from Privilege Style, May-September 2015,

Jet2.com 757-21B G-LSAH painted in Jet2's traditional silver (grey) and red colour scheme. (Author's Collection)

Jet2.com 757-23N G-LSAK was first delivered to American Trans Air in November 1996 before being bought by Jet2 at the beginning of 2010. (Author's collection)

Another 757-21B that was acquired by Jet2.com from China Southern Airlines is G-LSAI, seen here about to depart from runway 23L at Manchester Airport. (Author's collection)

Jet2.com 757-204 G-LSAL on final approach to Palma de Mallorca Airport. ('G-LSAL B757-204W Jet2 Holidays PMI 26May12' by Ken Fielding, licensed under CC BY-SA 3.0)

Boeing 757-236 G-LSAJ joined Jet2.com in May 2008 after operating for at least eight different charter carriers since 1990. (Author's collection)

757-204 G-LSAM was leased by Jet.com from Allegiant Air between March 2011 and November 2012. ('G-LSAM' by Mark Winterbourne, licensed under CC BY-SA 2.0)

CHAPTER 5: BRITAIN'S LAST OPERATOR OF PASSENGER 757S: JET2.COM AND THE BOEING 757

Jet2.com 757-2K2 G-LSAN was the final 757 to be acquired by Jet2, in May 2012. (Jet2.com)

Jet2.com wet-leased 757-256 EC-ISY from Spanish charter airline Privilege Style for the 2015 summer season. (Author's collection)

757-236 G-POWH was leased by Jet2.com from Titan Airways to provide additional capacity during the 2016 and 2018 summer seasons. ('Titan Airways Jet2 Boeing 757-200 G-POWH' by Michael Oldfield, licensed under CC BY-SA 4.0)

Chapter 6:

The Flexible Freighter

Three main variants of the 757 freighter have been produced:
- Boeing 757-200PF (Package Freighter)
- Boeing 757-200M
- Boeing 757-200 SF/PCF

Boeing 757-200PF

During 1985 Boeing became aware of a potential market for a dedicated 757 freighter. It emerged from a survey of the overnight express package delivery business in the US. Boeing targeted a number of the leading freight carriers, including Flying Tigers, FedEx, United Parcel Service (UPS) and DHL. UPS were particularly attracted to the potential offered by a 757 freighter, in particular the low noise levels of its engines for night operations. There was also interest from the US Post Office. The 757-200PF (Package Freighter) was announced on 30 December 1985 when UPS placed an order for twenty freighter versions, plus fifteen options. Ten of the options were taken up in March 1989 and a further twenty aircraft, plus forty-one options, were ordered by the carrier in November 1990, with delivery scheduled through to the end of 2001.

The 757-200PF differs from the 757-200 passenger version in that it has no cabin doors, windows or interior passenger amenities. Access to the cockpit is through a small crew entry door or 'hatch' (22 x 55in; 1.8 x 2.56m) in place of the normal forward loading door. The door is fitted on the port side of the aircraft near the cockpit window, forward of the position of the main passenger entry door on the passenger version. A large, upward opening main-deck cargo door (134 x 86in; 3.4 x 2.2m) is installed on the port side of the forward fuselage, between the leading edge of the wing and the flight crew compartment, for bulk loading and unloading of standard cargo containers (typically 124in x 88in). The aircraft has a smaller cockpit than the passenger 757-200; the main deck fuselage interior is lined with a smooth fibreglass finish and optimised for the transport of freight. There is a solid bulkhead with a sliding door at the front end of the main deck which acts as a restraint wall between the flight deck and the main cargo deck.

The 757-200PF has a maximum take-off weight of 255,000lb (115,660kg) and, when fully loaded, a maximum range of up to 3,150nm (5,830km). The maximum revenue payload capability is 87,700lb (39,780kg) including the container weight. The volume of the main deck is 6,610 ft3 (187m3); it is capable of accommodating up to 15 standard-size ULD containers or pallets. This is supplemented by two lower deck holds - one forward of the wings, one behind the wings - which provide an additional 1,830 ft3 (51.8m3) of space for bulk cargo. The lower holds can be fitted with a telescoping baggage system to load custom-fitted cargo modules. The aircraft is powered by either Pratt & Whitney PW2037 or PW2040 turbofans (the latter providing up to 12% more thrust), or Rolls-Royce RB.211-535E4B engines.

As the 757-200PF does not carry passengers, it can operate transatlantic flights independent of ETOPS requirements. Nevertheless, aircraft operated by UPS on extended range, trans-oceanic flights do feature some modifications, including an upgraded APU, additional cargo bay fire suppression, a backup hydraulic motor generator and an enhanced EICAS system. The UPS 757-200PFs also have the option for an auxiliary fuel tank to be installed in the forward section of the rear lower cargo hold, providing an additional 3,030-3,410l (800-900 gallons) of fuel.

The first 757-200 PF was rolled out at Boeing's Renton site on 15 July 1987. UPS received its first two aircraft on 16-17 September 1987 and went on to take delivery of seventy-five aircraft, designated 757-24APF, all of which remain in service today. A total of eighty 757-200PFs were built at Renton. The other initial operators of the 757-200PF included: Challenge Air Cargo, who took delivery of two aircraft in July 1989 and September 1990, Zambia Airways, who leased one aircraft in October 1990 for three years from Ansett

Boeing 757-24APF N430UP was delivered to UPS in October 1992. ('N430UP' by Jeroen Stroes Aviation Photography, licensed under CC BY-SA 2.0)

Ethiopian Airlines was the first non-US operator of the 757-200PF. The carrier acquired a single aircraft, registered ET-AJS, in August 1990. (Pertti Sipilä)

Challenge Air Cargo acquired three 757-23APFs between July 1989 and September 1992 including N573CA. ('Challenge Air Cargo Boeing 757-23APF; N573CA@ MIA;31.01.1998 by Aero Icarus, licensed under CC BY-SA 2.0)

Boeing 757-23APF 9J-AFO operated for Zambia Airways for three years from October 1990. The aircraft was sadly lost in July 2002 while operating for DHL, when it was involved in a mid-air collision with a Tupolev TU-154M over Überlingen, Germany. (John Visanich)

Worldwide, Ethiopian Airlines, who acquired a new aircraft in August 1990 and operated it until June 2018 and former British operator, Anglo Cargo, who received its sole 757-200PF on lease from Ansett Worldwide in August 1991.

In addition to UPS, current operators of the 757-200PF are Icelandair, Asia Pacific Airlines, Swiftair and DHL Austria. The former Zambia Airways aircraft crashed near Überlingen, Germany in July 2002 while operating for DHL, following a mid-air collision with a Tupolev TU-154M due to an air traffic control error.

Boeing 757-200M

The Boeing 757-200M (sometimes referred to as the 757-200C) is a convertible or 'combi' freighter which is capable of carrying a combination of freight and passengers on the fuselage main deck in a mixed configuration. A main cargo door, similar to that installed on the 757-200PF, is fitted on the port side of the fuselage, forward of the wing. All windows, cabin doors and the cabin interior are retained from the passenger 757-200. The initial variant could carry 2-4 freight pallets or cargo containers (a maximum of nine tons of cargo) and between 123 and 148 passengers, or be relatively quickly converted to carry a full passenger load. In the mixed mode, the cargo was carried in the forward section of the main deck, separated from the passengers by a moveable partition.

There was very little interest in the 757-200M from freight operators and only one aircraft was built for Royal Nepal Airlines (Nepal Airlines since 2007). The aircraft made its first flight on 15 July 1988 and entered into service in September of the same year. Nepal Airlines operated the aircraft out of Tribhuvan International Airport in the foothills of the Himalayas

Only one 757-200M Convertible or 'Combi' freighter was built and delivered to Royal Nepal Airlines in September 1988, registered 9N-ACB. ('Nepal Airlines 757-200M 9N-ACB' by Toby Lam, licensed under CC BY-SA 2.0)

The first Boeing 757-200 to undergo a passenger to passenger/cargo combi conversion by ST Aerospace, seen here operating for TNT Airways in February 2016 as OO-TFA. ('Uno de esos aviones bien raros' by Javier Rodríguez, licensed under CC BY-SA 2.0)

Royal New Zealand Air Force Boeing 757-2K2 NZ7571 at the 2015 Australian International Airshow. ('RNZAF (NZ7571) Boeing 757-2K2 at the 2105 Australian International Airshow' by Bidgee, licensed under CC BY-SA 3.0 au)

Boeing 757-28A(SF) standard freighter OE-LFE operating for ASL Airlines Belgium. This aircraft was converted from 757-28A(C) Combi freighter OO-TFA between 2018 and 2020. All the cabin windows are now filled compared with the same aircraft in the previous image. (Felix Goetting)

until the end of September 2018, when it was sold to CSDS Aircraft Sales and Leasing. While operating for Nepal Airlines it was powered by Rolls-Royce RB.211-535E4B engines and had a maximum take-off weight of 240,000lb (110,000kg).

In April 2007, Singapore Technologies Aerospace (ST Aerospace), through its subsidiary, VT Mobile Aerospace Engineering based in Alabama, began the conversion of two former passenger 757-200s into 757-200 combi freighters for the Royal New Zealand Air Force. The two 757s had previously operated for ten years for charter carrier Transavia Airlines from February and May 1993 respectively before being sold to the Royal New Zealand Air Force in April/June 2003. The intention of the Air Force was to have the aircraft converted into a combined freight-passenger configuration so they could be used in a flexible, multi-purpose role. The conversion work included installing a main deck cargo door and fitting a strengthened floor for the carriage of large and heavy cargo (with a capability to carry eleven cargo pallets). There was a new cargo handling system, an avionics update, additional in-built air stairs

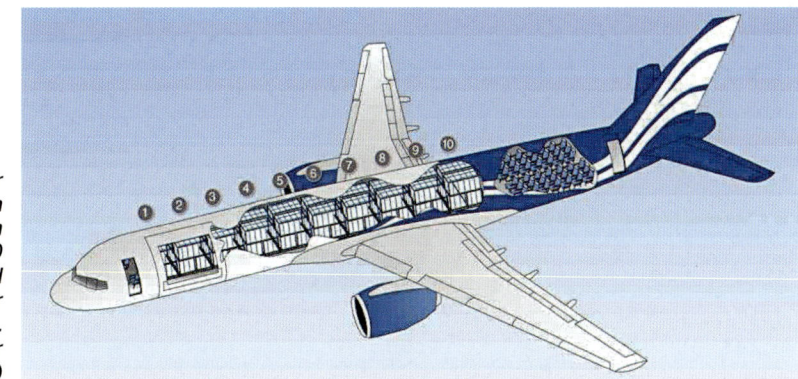

Pemco's passenger to combi conversion programme began in 2010, with 10 pallet positions and a 46 seat passenger compartment. (Pemco World Air Services)

Former Avianca 757-2Y0 EI-CEZ which was converted by Pemco World Air Services to a 757-2Y0(C) Combi configuration in 2012 and is currently owned by Air Transport International (N754CX). It is seen here operating for the U.S. Air Force. (Roland Balik)

Illustration of Precision Aircraft Solutions' 757-200 Precision Conversion Combi (PCC). (Zach Young, Precision Aircraft Solutions)

on one of the rear passenger doors and a flight crew boarding ladder in the nose wheel bay for operations from remote airfields without any infrastructure. The completed aircraft were delivered to the Royal New Zealand Air Force in August 2008 and February 2009.

In December 2010, ST Aerospace (again using subsidiary VT Mobile Aerospace Engineering) was selected by Guggenheim Aviation Partners to complete a passenger aircraft to passenger/cargo combi conversion on a 757-200; its first conversion for a commercial customer. The combi configuration provided capacity for eight containers in the forward section of the main deck and up to eighty passengers in the rear cabin section, located behind the wing. The first conversion was completed on a former Air Finland 757-200 (OH-AFK), which was acquired by Guggenheim Aviation Partners in March 2011 and converted to a 757-200 combi for use by TNT Airways. In May 2016 the aircraft was moved on to ASL Airlines Belgium before being withdrawn from service at the end of 2018 and converted into a full standard freighter configuration by ST Engineering, re-entering service in October 2020.

VT Mobile Aerospace Engineering also entered into an agreement with North American Airlines in December 2010 for the conversion of some of its fleet of ten 757-200 passenger aircraft to a combi configuration. However, the conversions were never started and Global Aviation Holdings, the parent company of North American Airlines, filed for bankruptcy in November 2013, selling North American Airlines' assets the following year.

Pemco World Air Services began to convert five former passenger 757-200s to a combi configuration for National Airlines in mid-2010. The combi configuration included installation of a large cargo door and freight handling system, provision of a cargo compartment with ten pallet positions and an automatic fire detection and suppression system, a forty-six seat passenger compartment with an in-flight entertainment system, four emergency exits and two full galleys. The payload was about 72,000lb (32,600kg) and the range similar to the passenger specification. In the end, only four conversions were completed and received FAA certification in Spring 2011. Three of the aircraft were sold to the Air Transport Services Group in 2013.

Another US-based aerospace engineering company, Precision Aircraft Solutions, launched a 757 passenger to combi conversion programme in October 2010. The Precision Conversion Combi (PCC) features a cargo compartment with up to ten full cargo positions (over 50,000lb cargo capacity), a main cargo door, a rigid barrier between the cargo compartment and the passenger compartment with an access door, together with a passenger compartment with seating for up to 54 passengers, a galley and four exit doors. There are several differences compared to the other Combis, including a small crew entry door on the left hand side of the forward fuselage immediately behind the cockpit window, similar to the 757-200PF, consequently the aircraft has no standard forward entry door. It is also the only 757-200 combi to include winglets. FAA certification for the Precision Aircraft Solutions conversion programme was gained in May 2013 and the company's first conversion, a former Aeromexico and SunExpress 757-200, entered into service with Air Transport International in June 2013.

Precision Aircraft Solutions' first Precision Conversion Combi (757-2Q8PCC) which entered into service with Air Transport International in June 2013. Note the blended winglets. (Zach Young, Precision Aircraft Solutions)

The passenger compartment and view through to the main cargo compartment of Air Transport International's 757-2Q8PCC. (Zach Young, Precision Aircraft Solutions)

The main cargo compartment of Air Transport International's 757-2Q8PCC, with the large cargo door on the centre right of the image. (Zach Young/ Precision Aircraft Solutions)

Boeing 757-200 SF/PCF

Boeing 757-236(SF) G-BIKP was the first 757 Special Freighter received by DHL following a Passenger-to-Freighter (P2F) conversion of the ex-British Airways airliner, completed by Boeing Airplane Services. ('G-BIKP' by Eric Salard, licensed under CC BY-SA 2.0)

The third type of 757 freighter aircraft involves the direct conversion of a passenger 757-200 into a pure freighter, a so-called P2F conversion. This type of conversion has been carried out by a range of companies, including Boeing who initially proposed and developed the idea in an attempt to gain business from major freight carriers such as DHL and FedEx. All these conversions involve the installation of a main cargo door on the port side forward fuselage, which is identical to that used on the 757-200PF aircraft. In addition, most conversions involve the sealing of all cabin doors (except the two forward boarding and galley doors and the adjacent lobby), as well as the plugging of the cabin windows, the removal of cabin passenger furnishings and amenities (e.g. galleys, seats, toilets, over-head lockers), the structural reinforcement of sections of the main deck floor and the fitting of a cargo handling systems, such as roller tracks. Due to the location of the cargo bulkhead on the 757, the main cargo deck had the capacity for fourteen standard pallets and one smaller container. Supplemental Type Certificates (STC) were issued for each, slightly different, conversion configuration.

The first batch of these conversions were completed by Boeing Airplane Services at its Wichita site and involved thirty-four 757-200s purchased from British Airways in 1999. The converted aircraft were destined for DHL International and their subsidiary, European Air Transport Leipzig (EAT). A number of partners assisted Boeing with subsequent conversions, including Israel Aerospace Industries (IAI) and ST Aerospace.

The new P2F freighter was designated the 757-200SF (Special Freighter) and the first converted aircraft made its maiden flight on 15 February 2001. DHL Aviation (UK) received its first 757-200SF on 10 January 2002 and it entered into service later that month. The freighter was capable of carrying up to 60,000lb of cargo.

In 2007, ST Aerospace, together with subsidiary VT Mobile Aerospace Engineering, agreed a seven-year deal with FedEx to convert eighty-seven passenger 757-200s to 757-200SF freighters (the contract was later increased to 119 freighters). The

Loading a DHL Boeing 757 freighter through the main cargo door. ('Boeing 757 DHL Loading cargo' by Curimedia, licensed under CC BY-SA 2.0)

conversions were completed using the supplemental type certificate owned by ST Aerospace and were based on Boeing's licensed passenger and freighter data. FedEx introduced the first 757-200SF into its fleet in July 2008 and all aircraft had been delivered by mid-2015.

Alcoa-SIE Cargo Conversions developed a second P2F conversion design in 2005 called the 14Plus 757-200 conversion, which resulted in a 757-200ASF configuration. This configuration involves a less complex conversion and retains most of the 757-200s original structure and systems, resulting in a quicker conversion at lower cost. It features almost 8,200 ft3 of cargo space providing 97% of the pallet volume of a fifteen pallet configuration and a structural payload of up to 72,000lb. The 14Plus configuration received an FAA supplemental type certificate in October 2006. The first 757-200ASF was delivered to Babcock and Brown Aircraft Management in January 2007.

Pemco World Air Services acquired the 757-200 freighter conversion operations and assets of Alcoa-SIE Cargo Conversions in 2010, including the supplemental type certificate. Subsequently, the 14Plus 757 conversion programme was marketed and completed as a Pemco product.

In 2001, Precision Conversions (later renamed Precision Aircraft Solutions) was established as a new company by Erickson Air-Crane, specifically to design, develop and gain certification of a fifteen pallet 757-200 passenger to freighter conversion programme. It produced the 757-200PCF. The main external difference of this version is the removal of the main forward passenger doors and their replacement with a small crew door, similar to that used on the

FedEx Boeing 757-2Y0SF N974FD was converted to a freighter from former Thomson Airways 757-2Y0 G-OOOX by ST Aerospace and delivered to FedEx in December 2012. ('FedEx, N974FD, Boeing 757-2Y0 SF' by Anna Zvereva, licensed under CC BY-SA 2.0)

FedEx Boeing 757-23ASF N918FD converted from a passenger-carrying 757 by Alcoa-SIE Cargo Conversions using a P2F conversion design called the 14Plus 757-200 conversion. ('FedEx, N918FD, Boeing 757-23A SF' by Anna Zvereva, licensed under CC BY-SA 2.0)

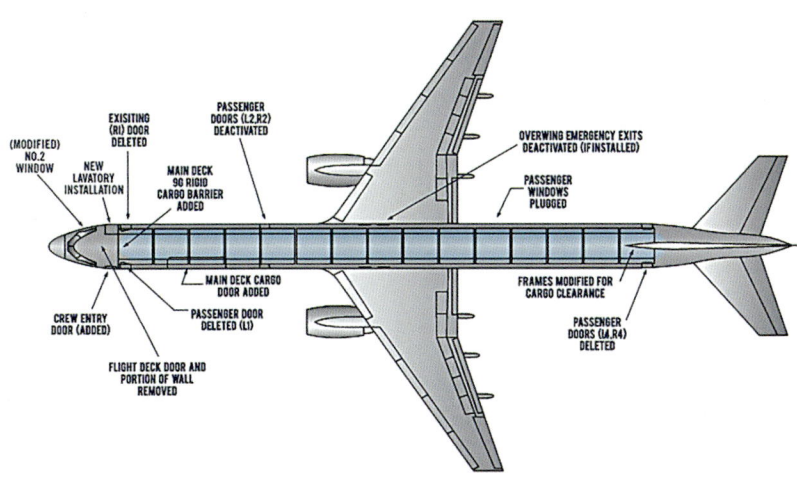

Plan of a 757-200PCF following a passenger-to-freighter conversion by Precision Aircraft Solutions. (Zach Young/Precision Aircraft Solutions)

757-200PF. It also features a main deck cargo compartment with a reinforced floor structure, and positions for fifteen standard pallets or thirteen larger pallets or containers, an ANCRA cargo handling system and a rigid 9G barrier between the flight deck and the cargo compartment. The main cargo door is operated from an independent, self-contained hydraulic system which is powered by the aircraft's electrical system rather than being integrated into the aircraft's main hydraulic system. The 757-200PCF is claimed, by Precision Aircraft Solutions, to have the highest available payload (up to 84,000lb) of any 757 freighter conversion and the lowest operating empty weight, at 115,000-116,000lb. This conversion configuration received an FAA supplemental type certificate in 2005 and, subsequently, over 150 757-200s have been converted to 757-200PCFs by Precision.

In early 2016, ST Aerospace/VT Mobile Aerospace Engineering received a supplemental type certificate for a fifteen pallet passenger-to-freighter conversion. The initial order for five conversions from SF Airlines was completed in 2018.

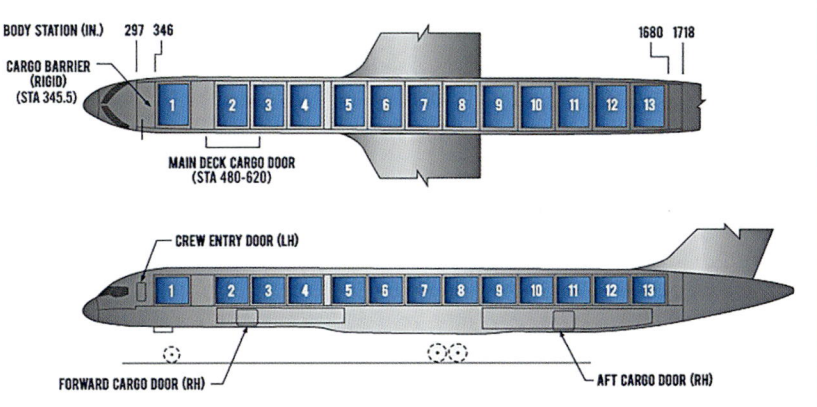

Configuration of a 757-200PCF for carrying thirteen large pallets or containers (Zach Young/Precision Aircraft Solutions)

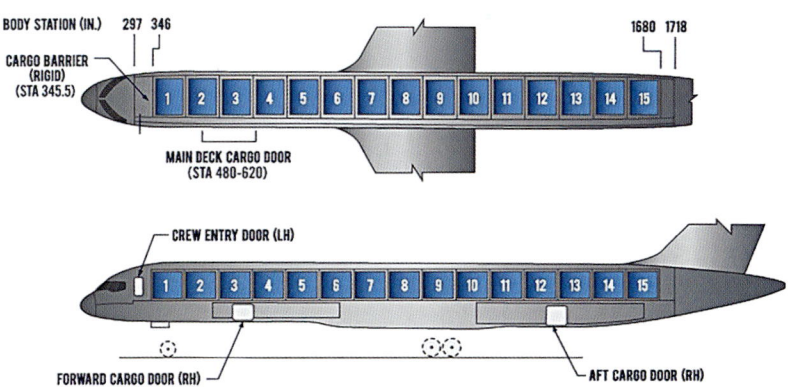

Configuration of a 757-200PCF for carrying fifteen standard pallets. (Zach Young/Precision Aircraft Solutions)

CHAPTER 6: THE FLEXIBLE FREIGHTER

Conversion of a passenger 757 to a freighter being undertaken by Precision Aircraft Solutions. (Zach Young/Precision Aircraft Solutions)

Boeing 757-223PCF of Cargojet Airways. The P2F conversion of former American Airlines 757-223 N647AM was undertaken by Precision Aircraft Solutions (Zach Young/Precision Aircraft Solutions)

The main cargo deck of a Boeing 757-200PCF. (Zach Young/Precision Aircraft Solutions)

Boeing 757-2B7(PCF) B-205S of SF Airlines. The aircraft is a 15 pallet freighter following the conversion of former American Airlines 757-2B7 N941UW by ST Aerospace in 2018. ('B-205S@PEK' by N509FZ, licensed under CC BY-SA 4.0)

Chapter 7:

The 757 as an Experimental Test Bed

The Airborne Research Integrated Experiments System (ARIES)

The first production 757-200 to be built was acquired by NASA in March 1994. It had previously been used in the 757 flight test programme before being operated by Eastern Air Lines from August 1983 (registered as N501EA). On delivery to the Langley Research Centre in Virginia in May 1994, it was re-registered as N557NA and slightly modified before being used in a variety of research and development projects, including an investigation of the electromagnetic environment in and around aircraft as part of the High Intensity Radiated Field Programme, the evaluation of a hybrid laminar flow control system for improving cruise fuel consumption and testing the avionics system for the proposed Northrop YF-23 Advanced Tactical Fighter. It also contributed to the development of the Boeing 777 fly-by-wire control system.

Extensive modifications to the aircraft ensued as it was prepared for its primary role as an airborne platform for the development and testing of new technologies aimed at enhancing and improving aviation safety. An experimental laboratory called the Transport Research System was established in the former passenger cabin of the aircraft. The laboratory included computers, data collection systems, fourteen research workstations and other hardware for monitoring and supporting research experiments and tests. The left-hand position on the flight deck was converted to a Flight Deck Research Station for the evaluation of flight systems and procedures. Eventually, an integration flight deck was established in the cabin which closely resembled, and was coupled with, the forward flight deck and allowed the aircraft to be flown by experimental guidance, while the pilots monitored it for safety. A video camera mounted on the vertical stabiliser (and on other exterior positions when required) provided a forward view over the aircraft and monitored the behaviour of the control surfaces on the wings during flight. In December 1998, the upgraded 757 was named the Airborne Research Integrated Experiments System (ARIES).

In addition to the aircraft modifications, a ground-based laboratory, which replicated the Transport Research System on the aircraft, was established for the integration and pre-flight checking of hardware and software prior to flight tests.

CHAPTER 7: THE 757 AS AN EXPERIMENTAL TEST BED

The Airborne Research Integrated Experiments System (ARIES) Project 757-225, N557NA (NASA)

The ARIES Project 757 during an experimental flight. (NASA)

An experimental laboratory called the Transport Research System was established in the former passenger cabin of the ARIES 757. The laboratory included computers, data collection systems, fourteen research workstations and other hardware for monitoring and supporting research experiments. (NASA)

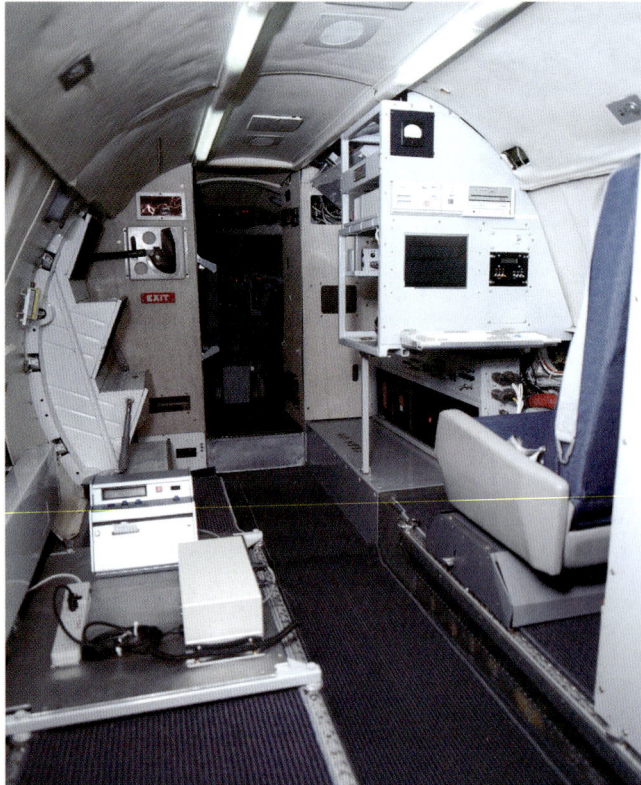

ARIES has been involved in a range of research projects for NASA including:
1. Low visibility landing and surface operations
2. Testing of a Runway Incursion Prevention System to improve the safety and efficiency of aircraft during landing, take-off and taxiing
3. The study of runway winter operations involving runway friction tests and braking performance when ice, snow and water are present on the runway surface
4. Testing of an airborne system aimed at reducing minimum separation during landing in low visibility conditions at airports with parallel runways
5. The use of GPS satellite data in carrying out automated landings
6. A study of the effects of jet engine contrails on the atmosphere
7. Evaluation of a radar system for detecting turbulence by measuring moisture in the air

The ARIES Boeing 757 left the Langley Research Centre in September 2006 for storage at the Dryden Flight Research Centre at Edwards Air Force Base in California. In April 2009 it was sold to L-3 Capital.

F-22 Raptor Flying Test Bed: 'Catfish'

In 1987, the prototype 757 (N757A) was first used as a testbed, flying up to two hundred hours to carry out initial in-flight testing of the avionics for the YF-22 Advanced Tactical Fighter Demonstrator, which was being developed by Lockheed, General Dynamics and Boeing. Various lobes containing sensors were fitted under the nose and rear fuselage of the aircraft, together with sensors on the starboard wing tip. Workstations installed in the cabin area of the aircraft for up to twenty-five software engineers and technicians allowed them to monitor and evaluate the avionics and to identify problems, some of which could sometimes be resolved during a test flight.

Following the selection of the YF-22 as the preferred advanced tactical fighter option in April 1991 and the award of a development contact for the F-22 Raptor, the 757 avionics testbed (or the Avionics Flying Laboratory as it was sometimes referred to) was prepared for further testing at Boeing's factory in Wichita, Kansas. An F-22 nose section (9ft; 2.74m in length) was fitted on the front fuselage section of the airliner containing a development AESA (active electronically scanned array) radar, together with other flight sensors. The aircraft was designated the F-22 Flying Test Bed, and its appearance with the modified nose led to the nickname 'Catfish'. A simulated and fully functional F-22 cockpit was installed in the cabin for operation of the test avionics. The Flying Test Bed first flew in November 1997.

In December 1998, a further modification was made to the 757 avionics testbed which involved the installation of a wing section or 'canard' with a span of 26ft (7.92m) on the crown of the aircraft, just behind the cockpit. It was known as the 'sensor wing' since it contained radar antennae and was fitted with a series of wing-mounted sensors for communication, navigation and electronic warfare systems that were to be used on the F-22. Testing began in March 1999 and continued through to mid-2006 as different stages in the development of the avionics software took place.

After two years in storage, the Flying Test Bed returned in June 2008 to test upgrades and enhancements to the F-22's radar and associated systems software. New flat-screen displays were installed at thirty workstations in preparation for the new phase of testing.

In 2017, the aircraft was involved in the testing of further upgrades to the avionics software in preparation for the introduction of new weapons on the F-22: the AIM-9X Sidewinder and AIM-120D AMRAAM air-to-air missiles. Its role as an avionics test bed is likely to continue for some time into the future following the award of the Advanced Raptor Enhancement and Sustainment contract to Lockheed Martin in November 2021.

Honeywell's Boeing 757 Test Bed

Honeywell Aerospace acquired a 757-200, registering it as N757HW, in April 2005 for use as a test bed for the research and development of the company's engines, avionics software and other electrical and mechanical systems. The 757 was originally delivered to Eastern Air Lines in February 1983 before being sold to Airtours International Airways in early 1995, then transferred to MyTravel Airways.

The aircraft has a distinctive pylon surrounded by an aerodynamic fairing protruding from the starboard forward fuselage on which engines can be mounted for airborne testing purposes. It also has a raised, blister-like feature mounted on the upper rear fuselage to accommodate various antennae

Prototype 757 N757A was used as a flying test bed for the Lockheed Martin F-22's avionics systems. An F-22 nose section was fitted on the front fuselage section of the airliner containing a development AESA radar and a wing section or 'canard' mounted on the crown of the aircraft, which led to the aircraft being nicknamed 'Catfish'. ('Boeing 757 Prototype N757A F-22 Raptor Systems Testbed' by Clemens Vasters, licensed under CC BY-SA 2.0)

Honeywell Aerospace acquired a 757-200 in April 2005, registering it as N757HW, for use as a test bed for the research and development of the company's engines, avionics software and other electrical and mechanical systems. (Adam Kress/Honeywell Aerospace)

Honeywell Aerospace 757 test bed N757HW testing a turbofan engine mounted on a pylon protruding from the starboard forward fuselage. ('N757HW Boeing 757 Honeywell Flight Test' by aeroprints.com, licensed under CC BY-SA 3.0)

and sensors. The cabin is fitted with monitoring equipment and a number of workstations. Although the cabin area is configured with twenty-five seats, a typical test flight usually involves a crew of seven to eight, including two pilots.

Since its initial flight with three engines in December 2008, the 757 test bed aircraft has played a significant role in the testing of the Honeywell HTF7000 turbofan engine series and the TFE731 turbofan and TPE331 turboprop engines in real world conditions. In addition, the aircraft has been used to test various technological developments, including advanced 3D weather radar systems, flight management systems, in-flight Wi-Fi and satellite communication connectivity. By mid-2022, the test bed had flown more than 800 flight tests, encompassing over 3,000 flying hours, and Honeywell has no current plans to retire it.

'Trailblazer': L-3 Communications 757 Test Bed

Former aerospace company L-3 Communications (now L3Harris Technologies) acquired an ex-Finnair 757-200 in November 2013 and registered it as N903TB. The aircraft had been operated, from new, by Finnair since October 1997. L-3 Communications named the aircraft 'Trailblazer' and, although its role isn't fully understood, it is believed to have been used as an avionics test bed. Some minor modifications to the aircraft, including the addition of two raised blister-like features on top of the fuselage, are thought to have housed antennae and/or sensors. In July 2018, the 757 was delivered to the United States Air Force and was assigned to the Special Air Mission fleet at Andrews Air Force Base, Maryland. It was re-designated as a Boeing C-32A and allocated the military registration 19-0018.

CHAPTER 7: THE 757 AS AN EXPERIMENTAL TEST BED

Boeing 757 ecoDemonstrator

Boeing's ecoDemonstrator programme was launched in 2012 with the primary aim of testing laboratory technologies which may have an environmental benefit in an operational environment. It included methods for improving fuel efficiency, reducing noise and gaseous emissions and decreasing the carbon footprint of airliner operations. As part of the programme, in collaboration with NASA and the TUI Group, a 757-222 (N506UA) was acquired from United Airlines in 2013, painted in a special 'ecoDemonstrator TUI livery' and registered N757ET. It was modified to investigate the effects of natural laminar flow and active flow control technology as potential ways for improving aerodynamic efficiency and thereby reducing noise and carbon emissions.

The wings of the 757 were modified to test several technologies for reducing insect residue contamination on wing surfaces, which creates drag, disrupts smooth airflow and can lead to increased fuel consumption. Retaining natural laminar flow over an aircraft wing can reduce fuel consumption by 6-15%. A variable camber Krueger flap was fitted on the left wing which, when deployed during landing, extended just beyond the leading edge. The flap was tested to see how effective it could be in preventing insect remains from accumulating on the wing's leading edge. An infra-red camera mounted on top of the fuselage monitored the air flow over the wing. On the right wing, a number of different non-stick experimental coatings which prevent insects from adhering to and accreting on wing surfaces were tested. The coatings were applied to panels on the second and third leading edge slats. The test flying was undertaken in different environmental conditions, mostly below 10,000ft where insects are abundant.

Boeing 757 ecoDemonstrator with a variable camber Krueger flap fitted on the left wing which, when deployed during landing, extended just beyond the leading edge. The flap was tested to see how effective it could be in preventing insect remains from accumulating on the wing's leading edge. (NASA)

The wings of the 757 ecoDemonstrator were modified to test several technologies for reducing insect residue contamination on wing surfaces. One approach involved testing a number of different non-stick experimental coatings which prevented insects from adhering to and accreting on wing surfaces. In the first part of the experiment, scientists collected bugs on untreated wing surfaces during initial test flights to establish insect accumulation rates. In this photo, taken after a flight, researchers count the number of insects to create a baseline against which to compare treated surfaces to see how effective the coatings were at reducing insect accumulation. (NASA)

The 757 ecoDemonstrator during a flight test to investigate active flow control over the rudder surface. (NASA)

The investigation of active flow control over the rudder involved the use of thirty-one active flow nozzles, called sweeping jet actuators, mounted on the right side of the vertical stabiliser ahead of the rudder's leading edge. The nozzles provided cooled, pressurised air on demand over the 757's vertical stabiliser and rudder surfaces, supplied by the auxiliary power unit via a heat exchanger to cool it. (NASA)

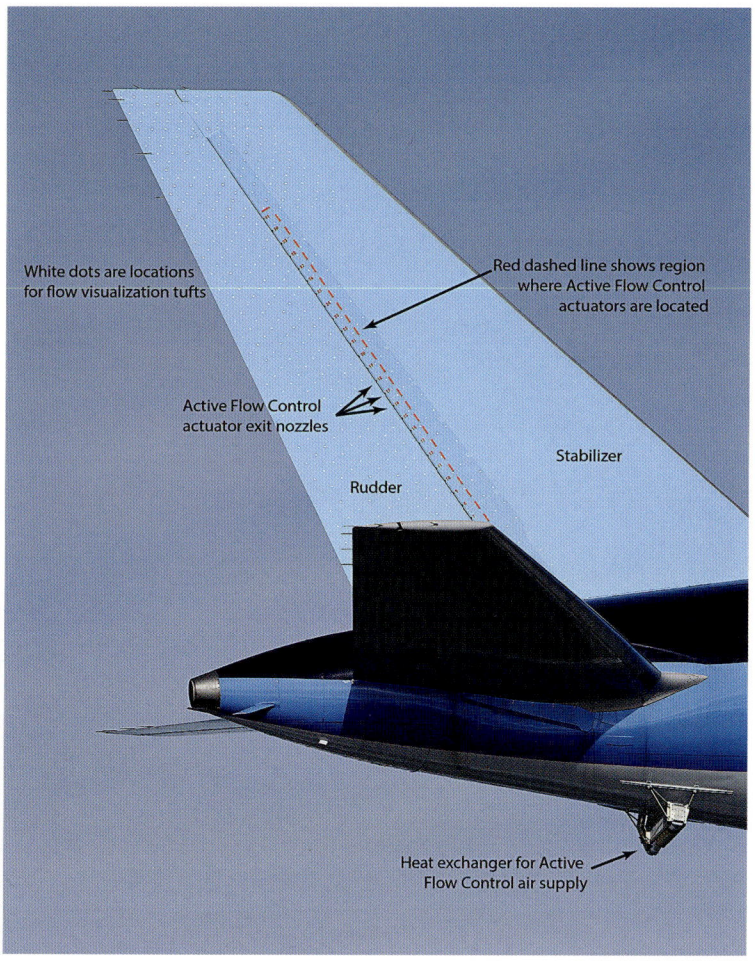

Tests completed on the vertical stabiliser of the aircraft involved investigating active flow control over the rudder in order to improve airflow and maximise aerodynamic efficiency. Thirty-one active flow nozzles, called sweeping jet actuators, were mounted on the right side of the vertical stabiliser ahead of the rudder's leading edge. The nozzles provided cooled, pressurised air on demand over the 757's vertical stabiliser and rudder surfaces, supplied by the auxiliary power unit via a heat exchanger to cool it. Wind-tunnel experiments indicated that an increase in side force on the vertical stabiliser provided by active flow control could result in smaller vertical stabilisers. The flight tests appeared to support these findings suggesting that a smaller vertical stabiliser would lead to a reduction in airframe weight and drag and consequently a decrease in fuel consumption for future airliners.

The 757 ecoDemonstrator was withdrawn from use in early July 2015 and broken up two months later.

Chapter 8:

Military and Government 757s

The United States Air Force (USAF) operates ten specially configured 757-200 airliners under the designation C-32. There are two variants: C-32A and C-32B.

C-32A

The USAF has eight C-32A aircraft which are primarily used for providing executive transport for the Vice-President of the United States (using the call sign Air Force Two), the First Lady, Secretary of State and other congressional leaders or delegations. Occasionally, a C-32A serves as Air Force One, replacing the larger VC-25A on trips to domestic destinations unable to support the 747-derived aircraft, or if both VC-25As are unserviceable. A C-32A often flies as a back-up aircraft in support of Air Force One on long-distance trips. The C-32As are operated by the 1st Airlift Squadron of the 89th Airlift Wing based at Andrews Air Force Base, Maryland.

From May 1998, four 757-200s were significantly modified by Boeing at its Wichita plant to operate as C-32As. The installation of additional fuel tanks in the forward and aft cargo holds (each tanks hold 1,850 US gallons (7,000 litres)) increased the range of the aircraft to 5,000nm (9,260km). The aircraft have state-of-the-art military avionics systems and a GPS navigation system. Traffic collision avoidance and enhanced ground proximity warning systems provide advanced warning of possible air and ground threats and the aircraft are all equipped with infrared countermeasures systems. They are powered by Pratt & Whitney PW2000 engines and fitted with winglets for improved fuel economy. Externally the C-32As are painted in a blue and white livery, with 'United States of America' markings along the cheatline and a stars and stripes flag on the vertical stabiliser. They have a series of antennae and sensors on top of and underneath the fuselage for terrestrial communications, and two satellite communication radomes on top of the fuselage, which provide high speed, secure connectivity for highly classified material.

The passenger cabin is divided into four sections. The forward section includes a communications centre, galley, lavatory and ten business-class seats. The second section is a fully enclosed stateroom for use by the primary passenger. The third section contains a conference room and staff facilities, including eight business class seats. The rear section has thirty-two business class seats and facilities for staff and accompanying media. In 2018, a contract was awarded for the interiors of the C-32As to be slowly refurbished at a cost of $16 million per aircraft, wasteful spending according to a number of critics. The refit includes more luxurious accommodation including leather seats and wooden tables, replacement of the double business class seating configuration in the rear section of the cabin with a triple-seat configuration, new carpets and lighting and routine painting and cleaning.

Three additional C-32As were acquired by the 89th Airlift Wing of USAF between 2010 and 2012, followed by another aircraft in 2018.

C-32B Gatekeeper

Two specially modified 757-200 airliners powered by Rolls-Royce RB.211 engines, designated C-32B Gatekeeper, are operated by the USAF. There is a high level of secrecy around the specific operations carried out by these aircraft. Their role involves providing global airlift for US government crisis response activities and special operations. This may be through the US Government's Gate Keeper mission, a programme which provides support to foreign nations involving State Department Foreign Emergency Support Team Missions and classified special operations and intelligence missions, such as in response to terrorism incidents. The aircraft are operated by two units: the New Jersey Air National Guard's 150th Special Operations Squadron based at Joint Base McGuire, New Jersey, and the 486th Flight Test Squadron at Elgin Air Force Base, Florida.

A number of modifications have been made to the 757 for the C-32B role. The front of the passenger cabin has 45-48 standard airline seats. All cargo has to be carried in the rear section of the cabin as two enlarged fuel tanks occupy much of the below deck cargo hold which extend the aircraft's range to 6,000nm (11,100km). The aircraft has in-flight refuelling capability through a universal aerial refuelling installation on top of the front fuselage, behind the cockpit. Fitted retractable airstairs and an on-board winch-based cargo loading system are available for operations to remote locations with limited facilities and support vehicles. One or two radomes are installed on top of the fuselage to support an advanced satellite communication suite. The aircraft are unmarked, apart from serial numbers, and are painted all white.

The two C-32Bs are registered as 00-9001and 02-4452, although the serial numbers have been known to change on a regular basis. The younger of the two aircraft, 00-9001 (c/n 25494), was delivered new to Avianca in April 1994 and purchased by the USAF in November 2000. The other aircraft, 02-4452 (c/n 25493), was first delivered to Ansett Worldwide in February 1983. It went on to operate for American Trans Air and several private companies, including Kodiak Associates, before being acquired by the USAF in February 2004.

Several other 757s owned by the COMCO Corporation are believed to operate for the US Department of Defense in roles similar to the C-32Bs and they also sometimes display military serial numbers.

Royal New Zealand Air Force 757s

The Royal New Zealand Air Force (RNZAF) operates two former passenger 757-200s which have been converted to combi freighters (757-2K2), as described in Chapter 6. Their registrations are NZ7571 and NZ7572. Both aircraft feature a large cargo door, upgraded APU, retractable airstairs and enhanced civil and military communications systems. They are operated by No. 40 Squadron, a RNZAF transport squadron, and are used in a range of passenger and freight roles, including VIP transport (Prime Minister and staff from the Department of the Prime Minister and Cabinet), transport of military personnel, delivery of equipment and supplies, medical evacuations and humanitarian and disaster relief assistance.

A contract was awarded in 2022 to upgrade the avionics of the 757-2K2s by replacing the old CRT display screens with LCD flight displays. However, as a result of the increasing age of the 757-2K2s and the type of operations they have been deployed on globally, their reliability has declined over the past 5-10 years. Finding an appropriate replacement to carry out the various roles of the 757-2K2s is challenging but the aircraft are expected to be replaced in the late 2020s.

Government and VIP 757s

The US Department of Justice has operated two modified Boeing 757-200s since February/March 2015, mainly for transporting prisoners around the country's prison system. The aircraft (N119NA and N874TW) are all-white and have few markings apart from a serial number and the American flag on the vertical stabiliser.

The first country to use a 757 for transport of the head of state was Mexico. A 757-200, originally built for

United States Air Force C32A 98-0001 which was acquired in June 1998. ('U.S. Air Force, 98-0001, Boeing VC-32A' by Anna Zvereva, licensed under CC BY-SA 2.0)

United States Air Force C32A 19-0018 on final approach to Madrid Torrejon Airport, Spain. (Javier Rodriguez)

United States Air Force C32B Gatekeeper 00-9001 taxiing at Stuggart Airport, Germany in April 2018. ('00-9001 at STR' by Juke Schweizer, licensed under CC BY-SA 4.0)

C32B Gatekeeper 02-4452 was acquired by the United States Air Force in February 2004. It is seen here at Malta International Airport. (Shaun Psaila)

The Royal New Zealand Air Force operates two former passenger 757-200s which have been converted to combi freighters (757-2K2). Shown here is one of those aircraft, 757-2K2 NZ7571. (Pseudopanax)

Royal New Zealand Air Force Boeing 757-2K2 NZ7572 landing at Pegasus Airfield on the Ross Ice Shelf during its first flight to Antarctica in December 2009. ('WN 10-0063-004 - NZ Defence Force' by New Zealand Defence Force, licensed under CC BY-SA 2.0)

Eastern Air Lines but never taken up, was acquired by the Mexican Air Force in November 1987 and configured as a VIP aircraft for use by the President of Mexico. Its call sign was initially TP-01 (Transporte Presidencial 1) but in February 2016 it became TP-02 after being replaced by a newly acquired Boeing 787. The 757 was finally withdrawn from service in November 2018.

The Sultan of Brunei and the Brunei Government used a 757 as a VIP transport aircraft from December 1987 to September 1989. The 757-200 (V8-RBC) was originally delivered to Royal Brunei Airlines in July 1986 and operated for the carrier until its transfer to the Brunei Government. It returned to service with the airline in 1989 before being sold to Kazakhstan Airlines in October 1995. The airline never used the 757 and sold it to Air Finance Ltd. the following month. It was subsequently leased to the Kazakhstan Government. On 1 December 1997 the aircraft moved to Orient Eagle Airways and then to Berkut Air in March 2002. In September 2019, it was registered with the Kazakhstan Air Force (UP-B5701). However, throughout the period from December 1997, the 757 continued to be used as VIP transport by the Kazakhstan Government.

Boeing 757-200s have been used to provide VIP transport for the President of Argentina for over 30 years. The first aircraft was delivered as new to the Argentine Air Force in July 1992 and was operated by the Presidential Air Squadron as Tango 01 (T-01). It was involved in several incidents during its service before being withdrawn from use and put into storage in December 2015 after the Presidential Air Group was disbanded.

Following a change in the President of Argentina in December 2019, the new administration made efforts to return Tango 01 into service. However, significant storage corrosion of the fuselage and engines was

CHAPTER 8: MILITARY AND GOVERNMENT 757S

found during an overhaul of the 757. A decision was taken to replace rather than repair the aircraft and the Argentine Government completed the purchase of a 757-200 in VIP configuration from the C&L Aviation Group in April 2023. It is registered as ARG-01 and was delivered on 25 May 2023. The aircraft was originally operated by Iberia from April 2000 before being configured as a VIP transport and transferred to the US Funair Corporation in 2005. It was sold to Validus Aviation in January 2017. The new presidential aircraft is designed to accommodate up to thirty-nine passengers and has a master suite and two additional bedrooms. It is equipped with additional fuel tanks and winglets.

The Yemen Government purchased a 757-200 from Uzbekistan Airways in August 2016 to use as VIP transport. The aircraft underwent a refit and was painted in the Yemen government's livery prior to delivery. It was registered as 7O-VIP and used the callsign 'IYE1', before being withdrawn and placed in storage in October 2020.

The Saudi Arabian Government own a specially-equipped Boeing 757-200 (HZ-HMED) which is used as a flying hospital. The 757 was originally delivered to Ansett Worldwide Aviation Services in June 1994. After a period of storage it was acquired by the Saudi Arabian Government in March 1995 and converted to a mobile hospital, including medical apparatus, a laboratory, an intensive care unit and a satellite communications system for sending and receiving medical reports. On completion, it was delivered to Riyadh in March 1997. A specially trained team of doctors, nurses and medical technicians are assigned to run the mobile hospital, which provides medical support to the extended Saudi Royal Family and can respond to medical emergencies anywhere in the Kingdom from its base in Jeddah.

The Mexican Air Force acquired a 757-225 in November 1987 and it was configured as a VIP aircraft for use by the President of Mexico and the Mexican Government, using the call sign TP-01. The 757 was withdrawn from service in November 2018. ('TP-01 – XC-UJM Boeing 752WL Fuerza Aerea Mexicana' by aeroprints.com, licensed under CC BY-SA 3.0)

Boeing 757-2M6 V8-RBC was used as a VIP transport aircraft by the Sultan of Brunei and the Brunei Government between December 1987 and September 1989. (Gavin Hughes)

The former Brunei Government Boeing 757-2M6 V8-RBC eventually became a VIP transport aircraft for the Kazakhstan Government. It is shown here registered as UP-B5701 and being operated by Berkut Air on behalf of the Government of Kazakhstan. ('UP-B5701 Boeing B757-2M6 B752-BEC Berkut Air' by flybyeigenheer, licensed under CC BY-SA 2.0)

Boeing 757-23A Tango 01 (T-01) of the Fuerza Aérea Argentina (Argentine Air Force), which was operated for the Argentine Government from July 1992 to December 2015. It is shown here at Zurich Airport, Switzerland. (Rolf Wallner)

In April 2023, the Argentine Government purchased another 757-256 in VIP configuration for use as a Presidential and Government aircraft. It is registered as ARG-01. (SR-Planespotter)

Boeing 757-23P 7O-VIP of the Yemen Government. This aircraft was acquired in September 2016 from Uzbekistan Airways. It was withdrawn from use and placed into storage in October 2020. (Agil Suwandi)

Another VIP-configured Boeing 757-200 (N757AF) is owned by the Trump Organisation and was used by Donald Trump for transport across the US during his 2016 presidential campaign. The aircraft was first delivered to Sterling Airways in June 1991 before moving to Mexican low-cost airline, TAESA, in July 1994. In 1995 it was acquired by co-founder of the Microsoft Corporation, Paul Allen, and converted to a VIP corporate aircraft for his use. It was bought by DJT Operations (Trump Organisation) in June 2011. The VIP 757 is powered by Rolls-Royce RB.211 engines and can seat up to forty-three passenger. It is fitted with a master bedroom, bathroom, shower, guest room, lounger, dining room and galley. Almost every fixture in the aircraft cabin is 24-carat gold plated.

The Saudi Arabian Government own a specially-equipped Boeing 757 -23A HZ-HMED that is used as a flying hospital. (Niclas Rebbelmund)

VIP-configured Boeing 757-200 N757AF which is owned by the Trump Organisation and was used by Donald Trump for transport across the US during his 2016 presidential campaign. ('Trump Boeing 757-200 (N757AF) at McCarran' by Tomás Del Coro, licensed under CC BY-SA 2.0)

Chapter 9:

What next for the 757?

It is over forty-one years since the Boeing 757 made its maiden flight. Of the 1,050 aircraft produced between 1982 and 2004, almost 600 remain in service in 2024, but what does the future hold for the 757?

Over 90% of the passenger-carrying 757s are operated by five airlines: Delta Air Lines, United Airlines, Icelandair, Condor and Jet2. Delta has the largest fleet of 757s and has yet to make a final decision on the future of its aircraft. The carrier introduced the Airbus A321neo into service in May 2022, replacing 757s on some of its transcontinental routes. Delta has a purchase commitment for one hundred and fifty-five A321neos with delivery of the aircraft through to 2027. These will progressively replace the 757s, although the airline has indicated that it will continue to fly at least fifty 757s up to 2027 and the newer ones in the fleet are likely to continue in service with Delta until 2035.

United Airlines plans to retire its current fleet of sixty 757s by the end of the decade and has placed substantial orders for potential replacement aircraft, including Boeing 737 MAX 10s, Airbus A321neos and Airbus A321XLRs. The German carrier, Condor, currently has a fleet of only eleven 757-300s, the 757s having already been replaced by Airbus A320s and A321s on all flights from Hamburg. It is expected that the entire fleet of 757s will be retired this decade following orders placed by the airline in July 2022 for A320neo and A321neos, with delivery due to begin in the spring of 2024. Similarly, Jet2 has placed firm orders for fifty-seven A321neos since August 2021, the first example being delivered in May 2023. The A321neo has an almost identical capacity to Jet2's eight 757-200s and appears to be an obvious replacement for the type during the next 2-3 years.

Icelandair has decided on the A321XLR and A321LR to succeed its Boeing 757 fleet. It is expected to acquire four leased A321LRs from 2025 and thirteen A321XLRs are scheduled for delivery from 2029. The carrier has indicated that the 757 will be phased out from 2025, suggesting that 2026 may be the last year that the type is operated by Icelandair.

Production of the 757 ended in 2004 and Boeing has yet to develop a direct replacement option with similar performance characteristics. Boeing has considered redeveloping the 757 on several occasions but costs have always been prohibitive. In 2015, Boeing outlined its plans to launch a New Midsize Airplane (NMA), described as an all-new and more capable replacement for the 757 rather than taking the option of revising the 757 to include new engines and an updated wing design with improved use of advanced composite materials. The NMA concept airliner was initially proposed as a seven-abreast, twin-aisle aircraft, with size characteristics mid-way between the 757 and 767, offering 20% more range and a higher capacity than the 757-200. Two versions were suggested: a 225-seat variant with a range of 5,000nm (9,300km) and a slightly larger 275-seat example with a range of 4,500nm (8,300km).

In May 2020, Boeing suspended its NMA plans due to ongoing 737 MAX issues and the impact of the Covid pandemic on the aviation industry. Instead, Boeing began to reconsider a re-engined 757 - the 757-Plus - which would compete with the Airbus A321XLR. As well as being fitted with new engines and modern cockpit technology, the 757-Plus also needed to demonstrate better fuel efficiency, increased passenger capacity and a greater range in order to satisfy current market requirements.

By the following year Boeing returned to the NMA programme and was considering a shorter, narrow-body, 225-seat variant with a range of 5,000nm. This variant, with composite wings and fuselage but using existing structures, systems and engine technology, was seen as a direct successor to the 757-200/300. However, in June 2022, development of the NMA was suspended again pending further progress on the development of next generation engines and digital tools for the design, building and monitoring of commercial aircraft.

The Boeing 757 is doing well in the air cargo market. There are over three hundred and twenty 757 freighters in service and more than 75% of them have been converted to freighters from retired 757-200 airliners, the so-called PCF and SF variants. The 757-200 continues to be a popular option among narrow-body aircraft for conversion to a freighter (P2F conversion) - ten of these conversions were completed in 2019 and 2020, thirteen in 2021 and fifteen in 2022. By the end of April 2023 three conversions had been completed with at least eleven more planned to be carried out by the end of the year. Recent customers include YTO Cargo Airlines, SF Airlines and Cargojet. In March 2023, the AAR Corporation announced the purchase of nine, former American Airlines' 757-200s for P2F conversion. Two of the largest operators of 757 freighters, FedEx (with converted 757-200SFs) and UPS (with factory delivered 757-200PFs), have not given any indication that they intend to significantly reduce the number of 757s in their fleets.

A potential future competitor for the 757 P2F conversion programme is the Airbus A321-200. The first A321-200P2F converted aircraft was delivered for launch by Qantas Airways in October 2020 and the number of conversions is slowly beginning to grow. However, the mid- to long-term prospects for the 757 freighter appear to be positive. The P2F conversion of a growing resource of passenger 757s being withdrawn from passenger service represents a cost-effective and valuable long-term investment. The anticipated continued growth of e-commerce will require more freighters, with suggestions that over 1,500 conversions will be required through to 2041.

To prolong the lifespan of 757s as commercial airliners and freighters, Rockwell Collins, L2 Aviation and Boeing offer a flight deck upgrade involving the replacement of six CRT displays and some analogue instruments with three large format LCD screens, forming a Large Display System (LDS). The LDS provides more information to pilots and cargo operator UPS is currently upgrading its 757 fleet with the system.

An innovative future use of former passenger-carrying 757 airliners involves conversion to aerial fire-fighting platforms through a passenger-to-tanker (P2T) programme. The anticipated increase in wildfires globally which are attributed to a changing climate will increase the need for such aircraft. Singapore Technologies Engineering (formerly Singapore Technologies Aerospace) signed a contract with Galactic Holdings in 2022 to convert 10-15 passenger 757-200s. This will be the first time that the 757 has been used for such a role. ST Engineering is responsible for the full design and engineering process, conversion of the aircraft and certification of the new type. The conversion programme will include removal of seats, plugging of all windows, structural reinforcement of the fuselage and installation of two 13,250l (3,500 US gallon) fire retardant tanks. The aircraft will be fitted with a modern retardant dispensing system with a high degree of accuracy of delivery of the retardant. Release of the retardant will be through two sets of doors on the belly of the aircraft, one set forward and the other aft. The first 757-200P2T is expected to be completed in 2024. It will be one of the largest aerial fire-fighting platforms available, offering the ability to operate from shorter runways in remote locations and being more fuel efficient than its competitors.

It is highly likely that some future retired passenger 757s will reappear as test bed aircraft. A recent example is Excalibur, which is designed to be used as a flight test bed for systems under development and consideration for use on the UK-led Tempest sixth-generation combat aircraft and for supporting capability enhancements for the RAF's Eurofighter Typhoon and Lockheed Martin F-35B aircraft. The UK-based aviation services company, 2Excel, are responsible for the project, under contract from Team Tempest partner, Leonardo. Excalibur will act as an airborne demonstrator, flying laboratory and integrated validation tool for communications equipment, radars and sensors made by Leonardo and other UK aerospace companies and international partners.

2Excel have acquired two 757s to support the project: a former TUI Airways 757-200

The Large Display System (LDS) flight deck upgrade for the Boeing 757, designed and developed by Rockwell Collins, L2 Aviation and Boeing. (Rockwell Collins)

CHAPTER 9: WHAT NEXT FOR THE 757?

(G-BYAW) and an ex-Titan Airways 757-200 (G-POWH) which was re-registered as G-FTAI. The 757's performance characteristics are ideally suited to the role. It can carry a payload of 28 tonnes at 42,000ft and a cruising speed of Mach 0.8, and operate for up to eight hours flying time over a range of 3,900nm. The height of the fuselage above the ground provides ample room for the installation of equipment underneath the aircraft. The first 757 (G-BYAW) was taken apart, piece-by piece, and used for testing in order to gain the required knowledge to undertake the modifications and support certification of the second aircraft in preparation for completing the Excalibur flight tests. The nature of the external modifications which are likely to be made to the Excalibur 757 remain classified, although released concept images show it featuring a pointed nose to mimic the likely Tempest design and six external locations

A concept image of a 757 passenger-to-tanker (P2T) conversion (ST Engineering)

A concept image of Excalibur (2Excel)

Model of Excalibur (2Excel)

for sensors. The passenger cabin will be fitted with flight test equipment, computer and data recording systems, observer stations for scientists and engineers and a representative 'virtual' cockpit.

Finally, while the number of passenger-carrying 757 airliners is likely to decline significantly over the next five years, we can expect to see the Boeing 757 to continue flying in a number of other guises into the next decade and achieve a fifty year milestone of operational service.

The ex-757 of Titan Airways (G-POWH) which has been acquired by 2Excel, re-registered as G-FTAI, and will be modified into Excalibur ('Titan Airways Boeing 757-200 G-POWH' by BriYYZ, licensed under CC BY-SA 2.0)

Appendix 1: Boeing 757 Technical Specifications

	757-200	**757-300**	**757-200PF**
Length	155 ft 3 in (47.32 m)	178 ft 7 in (54.5 m)	155 ft 3 in (47.32 m)
Tail height		44 ft 6 in (13.56 m)	
Width		12 ft 4 in (3.76 m)	
Wingspan		124 ft 10 in (38.05 m)	
Wing area		1,994 ft^2 (185.25 m^2)	
Wing sweep		25°	
Cabin Length	118 ft 4 in (36.1 m)	141 ft 7 in (43.15 m)	111 ft 3 in (33.91 m)
Cabin Height		7 ft (2.13 m)	
Cabin width		11 ft 7 in (3.53 m)	
Seating	200 – 239	243 – 295	
Total cargo volume	1,670 ft^3 (47.3 m^3)	2,370 ft^3 (67.1 m^3)	8,405 ft^3 (238 m^3)
Zero fuel weight	184,000 lb (83,460 kg)	209,561 lb (95,255 kg)	200,000 lb (90,720 kg)
Max take-off weight	255,000 lb (115,666 kg)	270,000 lb (122,500 kg)	255,000 lb (115,666 kg)
Max Landing weight	198,000 lb (89.811 kg) – 210,000 lb (95,254 kg)		
Max fuel capacity	11,253 US gal (42.592 L)	11,490 US gal (43,490 L)	11,253 US gal (42.592 L)
Max Payload	57,160 lb (25,920 kg)	68,150 lb (30,910 kg)	87,700 lb (39,780 kg)
Cruise speed	Mach 0.8 (461 kn; 854 km/h; 531 mph)		
Range	2,460-3,915 nm	2,460-3,400 nm	2,460-3,935 nm
Ceiling	42,000 ft		
Engines (x2)	Rolls-Royce RB211-535-E4(B) Pratt & Whitney PW2037/2040/2043		

Appendix 2: Boeing 757 Orders and Deliveries

YEAR	ORDERS	DELIVERIES
1978	38	
1979	0	0
1980	64	0
1981	3	0
1982	2	2
1983	26	25
1984	2	18
1985	45	36
1986	13	35
1987	46	40
1988	148	48
1989	166	51
1990	95	77
1991	50	80
1992	35	99
1993	33	71
1994	12	69
1995	13	43
1996	59	42
1997	44	46
1998	50	54
1999	18	67
2000	43	45
2001	37	45
2002	0	29
2003	7	14
2004	0	11
2005	0	2
TOTAL	**1,049**	**1,049**

Appendix 3: Boeing 757 Timeline

1976	Boeing 7N7 design programme begins
February 1978	Boeing 7N7 becomes the 757
August 1978	Boeing 757 is officially launched with the announcement of 19 orders from British Airways and 21 orders from Eastern Air Lines
23 March 1979	Final approval for the production of the 757-200 is announced
13 January 1982	First Boeing 757-200, prototype N757A (c/n 22212), is rolled out at Renton, Washington
19 February 1982	Maiden flight of the Boeing 757-200, N757A, from Renton Municipal Airport. After a 2hr 31 min flight, the aircraft landed at Paine Field, Everett, Washington
22/28 December 1982	Eastern Airways receives its first two production 757-200s, powered by Rolls-Royce RB.211-535 turbofans
December 1982/ January 1983	The Rolls-Royce RB.211-powered 757 receives FAA and CAA certification
1 January 1983	The 757 begins commercial operations with Eastern Air Lines
25/31 January 1983	British Airways takes delivery of its first two 757-200s
9 February 1983	The 757-200 enters service with British Airways
14 March 1984	First flight of a 757 powered by Pratt & Whitney PW2037 engines
November 1984	Delta Air Lines begins commercial services with first Pratt & Whitney PW2037-powered 757s
31 December 1985	Boeing 757PF (Package Freighter) launched with order for twenty aircraft by UPS
17 February 1986	Royal Nepal Airlines place order for first 757-200 Combi
December 1986	The Rolls-Royce RB.211-powered 757 receives 120 minute ETOPS certification
16 September 1987	First two 757PFs delivered to UPS

Boeing 757 · Timelines

November 1987	Mexican Air Force receive a 757-200 configured as a VIP aircraft for use by the President of Mexico and become first military operator of the 757
September 1988	First 757-200 Combi delivered to Royal Nepal Airlines
March 1990	Pratt &Whitney PW2000-powered 757 receives 120 minutes ETOPS certification
July 1990	The Rolls-Royce RB.211-535E4- and RB.211-535C-powered 757 receives 180 minute ETOPS certification
April 1992	Pratt &Whitney PW2000-powered 757 receives 180 minutes ETOPS certification
September 1996	Boeing announces the launch of the 757-300 at the Farnborough Air Show
31May 1998	First 757-300 (N757X, c/n 29016) is rolled out at Boeing's Renton factory, with an order for 12 aircraft from Condor
2 August 1998	Maiden flight of the Boeing 757-300
January 1999	757-300 receives FAA and European Joint Aviation Authorities (JAA) type certification together with 180-minute extended range twin-engine operations (ETOPS) approval
19 March 1999	First Boeing 757-300 enters service with Condor
15 February 2001	The first converted P2F freighter, designated the 757-200SF (Special Freighter), makes its maiden flight
10 January 2002	DHL receives its first 757-200SF
14 February 2002	Boeing delivers the 1,000 757, N179AA (c/n 32397) to American Airlines
October 2003	Boeing announce the end of 757 production
27 April 2004	Last 757-300 to be produced (N56859, c/n 32818) is delivered to Continental Airlines. A total of fifty-five 757-300s were produced.
28 October 2004	The final 757 to be built, a 757-200 for Shanghai Airlines, rolls off the production line at Renton. It was delivered on 28 November 2005.

Bibliography

Becher, T., *Boeing 757 and 767*, The Crowood Press, 1999

Birtles, P., *Boeing 757/767/777* (3rd Edition), Ian Allan Publishing, 1999

Birtles, P., *Boeing 757*, Airlife Publishing, 2000

Dornseif, D., *Boeing 757*, Schiffer Publishing, 2022

Eden, P.E. (General Editor), *Civil Aircraft Today*, Silverdale Books, 2006

Falconer, Jonathan, *Modern Civil Airliners*, JJN Publishing, 2021

Norris, G. and Wagner, M., *Boeing*, MBI Publishing Company, 1998

Norris, G. and Wagner, M., *Modern Boeing Jetliners*, MBI Publishing Company, 1999

Pelletier, A., *Boeing: The Complete Story*, Haynes, 2010